# WINGS OF OPPORTUNITY

# WINGS OF OPPORTUNITY

## THE WRIGHT BROTHERS IN MONTGOMERY, ALABAMA, 1910

*America's First Civilian Flying School
and the City that Capitalized on It*

~

## JULIE HEDGEPETH WILLIAMS

*To LaRhonda Brown—
Thank you for all you
have done for both of our boys!*

NEWSOUTH BOOKS
Montgomery | Louisville

*Julie Hedgepeth Williams*

NewSouth Books
P.O. Box 1588
Montgomery, AL 36102

Library of Congress Cataloging-in-Publication Data

Williams, Julie Hedgepeth.
Wings of opportunity : the Wright brothers in Montgomery, Alabama, 1910 /
Julie Williams.
p. cm.
Includes bibliographical references and index.
ISBN-13: 978-1-58838-168-2 (alk. paper)
ISBN-10: 1-58838-168-4 (alk. paper)
1.  Flight schools—Alabama—Montgomery—History—20th century. 2.  Flight
training—Alabama—Montgomery—History—20th century. 3.  Wright, Wilbur,
1867-1912—Homes and haunts. 4.  Wright, Orville, 1871-1948—
Homes and haunts.  I. Title.
TL713.M66W55 2009
629.132'52071076147—dc22

2009026664

Printed in the United States of America
by Rose Printing Company

TO THE WRIGHTS IN MY OWN FAMILY:

JAN, JON, NATHAN, AND ELEANOR

# CONTENTS

# ACKNOWLEDGMENTS

I would like to thank Paulette Kilmer for admiring my paper about the Wright brothers' press relations in Montgomery enough to write me a letter of introduction for submitting it to an academic journal. That kindness made me realize I wanted to turn the paper into a book instead. And since I didn't want to disappoint Paulette, by golly I kept at it.

Many, many thanks go to Maxwell Air Force Base's Air Force Historical Research Agency (Montgomery, Alabama) for allowing me to use the bulk of the photographs in this book, which includes all but the photos of the Montgomery streetcar, the Tallassee Falls Power Plant, and Teddy Roosevelt's terrifying flight. Especially helpful at Maxwell were George Cully and Bonita Harris, along with Sylvester Jackson. I thank the very patient Brian Seidman and Randall Williams of NewSouth Books for putting me in touch with George and Bonita. Jerome Ennels was also encouraging and helpful in regard to the photos.

Bill Tharpe at Alabama Power Co. in Birmingham was so gracious to allow me to use the photos of the "Lightning Route" streetcar and the Tallassee Falls Power Plant, as well as to take my son Alden and me through the terrific archives at Alabama Power. Without such a personal tour, I'd have never spotted the photographs.

I could not have completed my research without the help of Elizabeth Wells and her staff in the Special Collections department of the Samford University library. I also want to thank Fred Fedler, who heard I was writing about the Wright brothers and sent along some interesting and humorous old newspaper clips about early airplanes.

I am also grateful to be able to use stills from the newsreel of the Teddy Roosevelt-Arch Hoxsey flight from Historic Print & Map Company of St. Augustine, Florida. I am indebted to my son Weston for figuring out how to make stills from the newsreel. In fact, I owe Weston more thanks for figuring out how to solve other photo technical issues. Thank goodness teenagers know how to use computers. A big hug to my husband, Evan, for patiently holding my hand for all these years of writing and editing, and to my sister Anne Hedgepeth for assuring me the book will go in her school library.

Ultimately, much credit for this book goes to my parents, Kay and Lloyd Hedgepeth, for bringing me into the world on Wright-Patterson Air Force Base in Dayton, Ohio, and raising me in North Carolina. Both places feel a keen sense of ownership and braggin' rights when it comes to the Wright brothers. When I found out the Wrights had spent time in my new state of Alabama, my parents' lifelong fascination with the Wright brothers made this book imperative.

# Wings of Opportunity

*A Wright Flyer glides over a Montgomery cotton field and
sharecropper houses in the spring of 1910.*

# THE YEARBOOK THAT NEVER WAS

T he first civilian school of flight in America did not leave a year-book. The class had a whopping five students, only three of whom graduated. The school featured no ivy-covered halls of learning. Instead, its classroom was an advertisement-covered building hawking the merchants and wares of Montgomery, Alabama. Students did not live in dormitories, but stayed, with the faculty, in a new hotel in downtown Montgomery. The school—which never really had a formal name—lasted only one semester in 1910. After three short months, the school packed up and moved to Dayton, Ohio, as the uncertain world of early aviation tried to progress from novelty toward necessity.

Despite the fact that the school was short-lived, its founder was one of the most significant names in the then short history of aviation: Wilbur Wright. Wilbur had decided in 1900 that he wanted to invent the airplane. As he wrote that year, he had been for some time "afflicted with the belief that flight is possible to man. My disease [his "affliction"] has increased in severity and I feel that it will soon cost me an increased amount of money if not my life."[1] Wilbur's determination to make history so specifically and his success in achieving his plan illustrate his genius and determination.

The Montgomery flying school's only professor was the most famous pilot up to that time: Orville Wright. Wilbur had had the original drive to invent the airplane, but Orville had quickly joined him on the project. In fact, it was Orville who piloted the first difficult flight at Kitty Hawk, North Carolina, on December 17, 1903. Wilbur and Orville had spent seasons from 1900 to 1903 in Kitty Hawk, first perfecting their man-carrying glider and then converting the glider into the airplane, or the "flying machine," as they called it. The jubilance of the four short but successful flights at Kitty Hawk in late 1903 linked the Wright name forever with the South. The brothers then took their invention home to Dayton, Ohio, where they perfected it over the next several years at their flying field, Huffman Prairie.[2] The brothers carefully guarded their invention, keeping it out of sight of both press and public, to protect pending patents. By 1910, with patents at last granted, the inventors and their successful Wright Flyer were still relatively unknown to the general public. There were, after all, only a few dozen airplane pilots in the entire world, and only a scattered few in America. Thus, it seemed a big step at the time for the Wrights to share their knowledge of flying and to expect others to carry on their work after them. The genius of flight would die with them if they could not impart it to others.

By late 1909, the brothers had taught about three dozen European men to fly, mostly in France. Wilbur had even operated a flight school for a handful of students in France in 1909,[3] but no American flight school yet existed for civilians. A trio of military officers was being trained in San Antonio, Texas, to fly the single Wright airplane the United States government had bought somewhat reluctantly.[4] The military pilots' training reflected the fact that the airplane was the newest instrument of war and—it was then hoped—prevention of war.[5] However, the Wright brothers foresaw non-military uses for the airplane. Passenger and airmail service were then being only dimly conceived, but it was clear that civilians wanted to fly. In 1910, flying was the ultimate sport, the pinnacle of fun for those daring enough and wealthy enough to buy their own airplanes. The pilots to be trained in Montgomery were expected to train sportsmen who would buy their own Wright Flyers.[6]

Another use of the airplane in 1910, though downplayed by the Wrights during their time in Montgomery, was to fly in exhibitions. Daring pilots would exhibit flight and create enthusiasm for it, thus creating a higher demand for airplanes. In the long run, the Montgomery flight school students gained most of their after-graduation notoriety and employment with the Wright Exhibition Team. In March 1910, as the Montgomery school got under way, the brothers formed the Wright Exhibition Company, with

Roy Knabenshue as manager. He had six years of experience promoting exhibitions of dirigibles at county fairs and would likewise promote Wright airplanes in similar venues.[7]

Although the Wrights had planned to train their student pilots at Huffman Prairie, it was typically cold and snowy in Dayton in the winter of 1909–1910. Wilbur accordingly went shopping for a location for a flying school in a warmer, more hospitable climate. He happened upon Montgomery, Alabama, in February 1910, and his brother set up the school there in March. The school stayed in session through May, when its graduates, near-graduates, and dropouts departed for Dayton.

The Wright school did have a campus. The school converted a cotton plantation, its perimeters lined with cabins of former slaves and their descendants, as the flying field. Thousands of Alabamians and others from elsewhere swarmed to the former plantation to watch the airplane in action. The Wrights' arrival was a sensation beyond the wildest dreams of forward-thinking Montgomerians seeking a way to rise above the deadweight of the Civil War, still lingering as a defining characteristic of the city's image. Montgomery itself, then, eagerly supplied spirit for the new school, with the city fervently hoping the school would become permanent.

The record of the first American school for civilian pilots was written at the time by the Alabama press, which fawned over founder, professor, student teacher, and student pilots in hopes not only of imparting information about airplanes and flight but also of publicizing the progressiveness of Montgomery, of Alabama, and of the South in general. The principal compiler of information on the flight school, a reporter for the *Montgomery Advertiser*, never signed his articles. It was not uncommon in the era for reporters to avoid signing their names, although that practice leaves us today wondering who this early and eloquent aviation reporter was. His record is entertaining and enlightening nonetheless.

There's no knowing how accurate the *Advertiser*'s reports were, although it is certain that the staff doggedly chased the story. The Wright brothers had had their troubles with the press of the day, which often resorted to guesswork in covering something as incomprehensible as the ability of a machine to fly. In fact, most of the Wright brothers' work had been misrepresented in the press for years. An unscrupulous telegraph operator alerted the press to Orville's private telegram to his father, announcing success in the first flights at Kitty Hawk in 1903. The next day, the nearby *Norfolk Virginian-Pilot* issued a largely made-up version of the story, based on the telegram and a lot of imagination. "Like a monster bird the invention hovered above the breakers and circled over the rolling sand hills at the command of its naviga- tor," the newspaper reported, "and after soaring for three miles, it gracefully descended to earth again and rested lightly upon the spot selected by the man in the car as a suitable landing place."[8] In reality those first flights were nothing like that—they never went over the nearby ocean; the Wrights were lucky to get the airplane to fly in a straight line, much less do maneuvers; and the longest flight that day was 852 feet, not three miles.[9]

The *Virginian-Pilot*'s flight of fancy unfortunately circulated far and wide via the Associated Press. The artist at Wisconsin's *Milwaukee Daily News* followed the Associated Press story to draw a picture of the first airplane in flight. He depicted the pilot sitting up in a contraption that looked something like a baby's playpen, when in reality the pilot lay prone on the wing, minus any sort of cage to hold him in. The artist depicted the motor as hanging below the wing, when in reality the motor sat upon the wing. The *News*'s drawing featured a fan-shaped rudder, something the Wright Flyer did not have, and the artist omitted the elevator on the other side of the airplane. Worst, he showed the propellers beneath the airplane, not at all where they were really located between the wings. One propeller, as the copy said, was mounted forward to help move the flying machine along. The other, as the artist showed it and as the erroneous copy reported it, blew upward, apparently to keep the airplane buoyed up in the air—or maybe to keep the canvas wings filled with air, as a hot air balloon needed to be filled with air. The public and the press understood hot air balloons, anyway. To add that personal touch, the artist drew the pilot in the familiar uniform of a sea captain, and because the *News*'s editor had trimmed out any descrip- tion of the airplane going over the ocean, the artist depicted it as hovering over a graceful river with a city below. For someone who had little accurate information on the airplane, the artist perhaps did fairly well in imagining a gigantic box kite that flew without a string. However, his mental image

*The famous first flight at Kitty Hawk, North Carolina, December 17, 1903. Orville was piloting from the prone position on the wing, while Wilbur ran alongside.*

was not complete enough to assure the airplane a proper landing—he failed to include the skids that the 1903 Flyer rested on.[10]

Such lavish guesswork so irritated the Wright brothers that they wrote a press release for the Associated Press to set the record straight:

> It had not been our intention to make any public statement concerning the private trials of our power "Flyer" on the 17th of December last; but since the contents of a private telegram, announcing to our folks at home the success of our trials, was dishonestly communicated

to the newspapermen at the Norfolk office, and led to the imposition
upon the public, by persons who never saw the "Flyer" or its flights, of
a fictitious story incorrect in almost every detail; and since this story
together with several pretended interviews or statements, which were
fakes pure and simple, have been very widely disseminated, we feel
impelled to make some correction.[11]

The release went on to describe the flight as it really happened.

The vexing incident was not a good beginning for Wright relations with
the press. The brothers, although they had been newspapermen themselves,[12]
seemed flummoxed by the false news, made-up "facts," and general bad
reporting. Perhaps their disappointment in the press indicated that their
own work as newspapermen in Ohio had had more integrity.

In any case, they quickly grew wary of poor reporting. In a fit of pique
about a *New York World* interview with early flight experimenter Octave
Chanute, Wilbur challenged Chanute on his incorrect statement in the
article that a critical principle of airplane control called "wing-warping,"
which the Wright brothers invented, had long been known before the
Wrights. Wilbur hoped it was just another case of bad reporting, "as this
opinion is quite different from that which you expressed in 1901 when
you became acquainted with our methods," he wrote to Chanute. "I do
not know whether it is mere newspaper talk or whether it really represents
your present views." Wilbur was devastated when Chanute replied, "This
interview, which was entirely unsought by me, is about as accurate as such
things usually are," and then proceeded to repeat the incorrect assertion that
the Wrights had not discovered wing-warping.[13] Although the disagreement
represented a personal crisis in a long-time professional friendship between
Chanute and the Wrights, Wilbur and Chanute did agree on one thing:
the press was unreliable. They both brushed off faulty news reports with
an "as usual" sort of treatment. Neither expected the press to tell the story
of flight accurately.

Even *Scientific American* couldn't get it right. The magazine, critiqu-
ing the Wright airplane in 1908 before the Wright brothers had formally
introduced it to the public, judged that if the pilot made one false move,

"the aeroplane would either plunge suddenly to the ground, or turn a backward somersault."[14] This, the Wrights insisted emphatically (over and over again), was impossible in a Wright Flyer, as it was basically a big glider with a motor. In a crisis, the Flyer would float to the ground, not plunge or somersault.[15]

The *Montgomery Advertiser* reflected the misconceptions, hopes, dreams, and fears about aviation in 1910, painting a picture of a time when flight was untested, unsteady, and unavailable to most people. Now, a century later, the *Advertiser's* coverage has formed the basis of this long-delayed yearbook for America's first school of flight.

*Confederate Memorial Day, April 19, 1886, at the Capitol at Montgomery. Jefferson Davis himself attended. But that was all in the past, as impatient and progressive young Montgomerians saw it by 1910.*

# RUNWAY TO THE FUTURE, 1910

For forward-thinking young men in Montgomery, Alabama, the arrival of Wilbur Wright in February of 1910 was an answer to prayer.

The Confederacy had crumbled nearly a half-century earlier, and some courageous young Montgomerians were suggesting that maybe it was time to move on. This proved somewhat unpopular, as there were many Confederate veterans still around who honored their role in defeat with ongoing pride.[16] The Ladies' Memorial Association in Montgomery had recently completed a monument to Confederate soldiers who had given their lives in the war for Southern independence; the cornerstone of the handsome structure had been placed by none other than Jefferson Davis.[17] The Daughters of the Confederacy were planning a convention to be held in Montgomery later in 1910.[18] The State Capitol was something of a shrine to Jefferson Davis, and his "White House" was located not far away.[19] It was hard to forget the past in a city that so revered the War Between the States.

Those who clung to the past were seeking to overcome humiliation via sectional pride, but for some of the younger set, it seemed the old-timers were *celebrating* humiliation—and that would not bring redemption. The future was indeed here; a new century was already a decade old, and it was time Montgomery and the entire South rose from the ashes of the dead system of slavery. The world was changing, and ambitious men in Montgomery saw the South as a potential leader in that change—if only their fellow Southerners would embrace the future.

Despite the dead weight of the Civil War, Montgomery had a head start in progressive leadership. In 1886 it had become the first city in the entire nation—maybe even in the entire world—with an electric trolley system. The public transport system whisked citizens around town in cars powered by an electric motor attached to wires overhead. The innovative electrical grid, installed by Belgian-born Charles Van de Poele, brought a big improvement over the mule-drawn trolleys of yesteryear. The electric cars sped along at an amazing six miles per hour, causing residents to nickname the system "The Lightning Route."[20] Eventually, bigger cities all over the globe would emulate Montgomery's electric streetcars.

Montgomery was rightfully proud of its electrification system and aware of its place in the world on that score. In fact, the city promoted itself as "The Electric City of Alabama." A star pupil at Montgomery's Barnes School, Roger Alston Jones, explained in an oratory contest in 1910 that the big electric jolt to the city came from Tallassee Falls, thirty miles away. A local company had dammed the Tallapoosa River and from turbines there supplied

*The future looked away from the Confederacy. "The Lightning Route" electric trolley system, arguably the first such system in the nation, was installed in Montgomery in 1885 and inaugurated in 1886. The photo above is at Court Square in the town center.*

*The Upper Tallassee Falls power plant was the first hydroelectric plant in the state and featured one of the first long-distance transmission lines in the nation. No wonder Roger Alston Jones was impressed. The plant is shown here after heavy flood damage.*

Montgomery with its dazzling electrical energy. Would-be power companies battled one another to become suppliers to the city, "and on account of the resulting competition Montgomery provides the cheapest light services of any city in the United States," young Jones remarked proudly.[21]

Other changes were also taking place, setting Montgomery on the path away from the Confederacy and on the electrified road to progress. In 1906, Montgomery's population had been 60,271, and by the dawn of 1910, the number had grown to 78,000. Of those, 5,000 were children enrolled in schools in the city. Roger Jones, the young orator, boasted that the city had some ninety factories and that the population was growing at about 10 percent per year, no small achievement. Ambitious citizens had coined a sort of citywide cheer, "100,000 in 1910," seeking even more population growth. Though that target hadn't been hit, to young Jones it was the happy challenge issued by society to his classmates, who, he said, "are the ones who will be Presidents and General Managers of large corporations, in place of our fathers, uncles and older friends. Montgomery is ripe with opportunities, therefore, all we boys have to do is to avail ourselves of them."[22]

One big advantage for Montgomery was its overall transportation infrastructure. There was that electric trolley system, and also the Alabama River, winding its way toward Mobile Bay, featuring new warehouses and a modern wharf at Montgomery. Dredges scraped the channel deeper and deeper for ever-bigger ships. Eight railroad lines snaked through Montgomery, reaching out to points all over North America. Montgomery County itself sported 175 miles of high-quality roads. All of these transport methods helped export Montgomery County's signature crop, cotton, which totaled 50,000 bales a season, as well as secondary crops of corn and timber.[23]

Perhaps the modern electrification had sparked it, but lately Montgomery had been sprucing up its appearance as well. Unsightly buildings on the city square had been replaced by a twelve-story First National Bank building and a new seven-story Exchange Hotel, which had the added attraction of being fireproof. Another twelve-story building, the Bell office building, was brand new, and a $250,000 wing was being added to the Capitol at the top of Dexter Avenue.[24]

These modern achievements notwithstanding, business leaders of Montgomery understood clearly that the city, state, and region had an image problem. Unlike the fresh-faced Roger Alston Jones, they knew perfectly well that the non-Southern public in general thought of Alabama as the cradle of the Confederacy, a hotbed of outdated thinking. The whole South was still under a cloak of suspicion from the Civil War, and the more the pity, as the region had fine weather and cheap electrification and good transportation and other positives in its favor, making it ripe for business ventures. Given the right public relations spin, the South could pull itself out of its negative image and join the progressive people of the world, taking its rightful place as a forward-thinking, forward-moving place for enterprise.

To that end, the *Montgomery Advertiser* newspaper was doing its best to tie Montgomery into a Louisiana publicity campaign to paint the South in a favorable light. In New Orleans' Mardi Gras celebration of 1910, an organization called the Progressive Union was actually bringing in flying machines to illustrate that the South was the land of the future. An Ohio aviator named McGill was to fly both a dirigible and an airplane over the admiring crowds at Mardi Gras. McGill's flights were to be the first by any type of aircraft in the South—at least, that's what the Progressive Union said, conveniently forgetting that Kitty Hawk itself was in a Southern state. But there had no doubt been few, if any, aviation exhibitions in the South. The Progressive Union also gave away free round-trip train tickets from various Southern cities to Mardi Gras. The organization bragged that Northerners were blizzard-weary and were discovering balmy winters in the South, and even though the free tickets did not reach above the Mason-Dixon line, the Progressive Union expected many Northern visitors to Mardi Gras.[25]

Certainly, those would-be Northern visitors to the Deep South needed desperately to understand the region. The South of 1910 suffered from a severe inferiority complex, and no wonder. Misconceptions about the area were deep and difficult to shake. An article in Boston's *Journal of Education,* for example, described horridly deficient education in Alabama, including windowless schools whose only light and air came from an open door. Boys sat on one side of the room and girls on the other, with rough-hewn logs for desks. The poorly paid teacher described in the *Journal* dressed raggedly and lived on a pathetic boarding plan, where she was fed "fried eggs that fairly swim out of the bowl in the fat they are cooked in." The article simply was not true, as various Alabamians protested,[26] but it reflected the image outsiders had of the state. In contrast, the *Advertiser's* agricultural writer, Gordon McKinley, rather hopefully compared the Montgomery farming community to the Garden of Eden, suggesting that the three feet of rich loam in the area must surely have been put there by God as part of the familiar story in Genesis. The middle part of Alabama was known as "The Black Belt," named for this rich, black soil, but, as McKinley grumbled, most people outside of the state assumed that the nickname meant the area was heavily populated by Negroes. He lamented that no one knew about the glorious agricultural texture of the area.[27] In fact, McKinley pretty much spelled out his opinion that Alabamians seemed to think of themselves as lesser beings. He commented that a project to grow kudzu to feed livestock was part of "the fight to awaken the State to a knowledge of its tremendous strength."[28]

A few halting gains were being made in building up Montgomery's and the South's depressed self-image. Montgomery Mayor Gaston Gunter was working on "a general 'city beautiful' scheme," the *Advertiser* reported. The scheme included clearing away blighted areas on the river bank, putting fine gates on the city cemetery, and widening some key streets.[29] In Congress, Alabama was fighting for the U.S. War Department to loan Confederate veterans five hundred tents and half as many saddles for a reunion to be held that April in Mobile. In another manifestation of Southern feelings of inferiority, however, there was quite a bit of jealousy that Union veterans had had many equipment loans for their reunions, but old Confederate soldiers had received no such consideration until now.[30]

Even more important than city beautification and a recognition of Confederate veterans, Montgomery was in line for a possible Army post. Again, jealousy marred this exciting development. There were lots of major Army posts in the East and in the central states, but there were no major posts in the South, a fact that illustrated Southern victimhood to many people. A military expert told the *Advertiser* that usually the Army decided to locate posts where citizens were mobilized to court the military—businesses, civic groups, and residents had to band together to furnish whatever the War Department needed. Citing an Army base's "commercial and developmental significance" to Montgomery, the *Advertiser* pronounced the quest for the post a "movement, perhaps, as important as any that has been launched in Montgomery in recent years." Montgomerians earnestly felt that the imminent opening of the Panama Canal would of necessity shift U.S. Army interests from Washington, D.C., southward, and Alabama wanted a piece of the action by getting that Army post.[31] Thus, local businessmen would have to pool their assets and good favors to turn the Army's head. Eventually those same Montgomery businessmen would have to band together in a similar way to lure the Wright brothers, so their preparations to woo the Army would turn out to be quite useful.

It was a hopeful time for a better future in 1910, especially with the Progressive Union in New Orleans trumpeting the good times just ahead for the South. M. B. Trezevant of the Union predicted:

The year of 1910 should witness the beginning of a movement southward, of the same character which, a few years ago, built up the great West to its present commanding position in agricultural and financial strength, and probably will result in turning the tide of American emigration to Canada toward our own country, where the genuine American has everything in his favor.[32]

Trezevant was confident that the signs of a population surge toward the South were already there. Newspapers and magazines were suddenly writing about the South, issuing special numbers about the region. *Collier's Weekly* was, like Trezevant, predicting that the South would be the next West. Upon hearing of *Collier's* upcoming issue on the South, Trezevant hurriedly wrote to the magazine to help cure false reports about the region. He vehemently denied the widespread belief that a warm climate was unhealthy. He also touted the largely unrecognized economic benefits of the South, which featured new prosperity and a welcoming attitude.[33] And, Trezevant might have added, the South was awaiting newcomers with modern thinking. The aircraft were coming to New Orleans, for example, and what could be more modern than aircraft?

Indeed, the readers of the *Montgomery Advertiser* were fascinated with the futuristic field of aviation, just then coming into the focus of public attention. The first United States air meet was held that January in Los Angeles. The Wright brothers did not fly in it, but other pilots were there, flying various types of airplanes and aircraft.[34] Roy Knabenshue flew a dirigible.[35] The French airplane pilot Louis Paulhan set a new record for height aloft[36] and was lauded for defying gravity.[37] Readers followed the meet and the aviators' exploits with rapt attention.

Airplanes and airships were hot items in everyone's imagination as the South pondered its step into the future. The *Montgomery Advertiser* was excited about both aviation and the publicity campaign of the Progressive Union and wound up linking the two. On February 2, 1910, *Advertiser* editorial cartoonist Gilbert Edge depicted the publicity campaign in the most radically modern way possible: He drew an airplane floating over the South, shining a spotlight down onto Alabama, with Montgomery itself

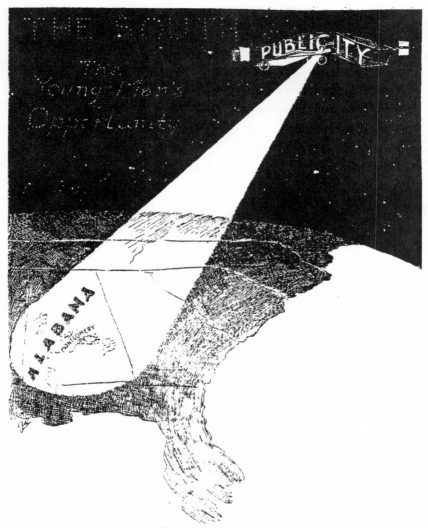

IT SHINES FOR ALL.

**Montgomery Advertiser** *cartoonist Gilbert Edge suggested that Montgomery needed to turn on some positive publicity. Although it was unthinkable at the time that an airplane would fly in the night sky over Montgomery, Edge drew one there. The unairworthy craft featured wavy, drooping wings.*

prominently lit—in fact, it was the only city he bothered to label. The stars in the night sky spelled out "THE SOUTH. The Young Man's Opportunity." Ironically, he cut New Orleans and Louisiana neatly out of the picture.[38] The Progressive Union would take care of that part of the South. Edge was urging Montgomery to step up to the challenge with its own positive publicity, the kind that would be needed to attract the would-be Army post.

In keeping with the popular concept of aviation as the leap into the future, Edge used the airplane only symbolically to illustrate Montgomery's part in the pro-South publicity campaign. The Progressive Union's campaign did involve the airships flying as entertainment at Mardi Gras, but certainly the *Advertiser*'s own version of the publicity campaign, as touted in the cartoon, would not really feature airplanes. No one in Montgomery expected to see an airplane any time soon, unless he or she got the free train tickets to Mardi Gras. Nevertheless, airplanes were the symbol of forward thinking, so Edge drew the map of the future-minded Southeast, with as accurate a biplane as he could muster, shining the beacon of publicity down on Montgomery. The airplane, labeled "Publicity," was badly drawn, featuring what appeared to be rather unbalanced and excessively drooping wings. Edge had never seen a real airplane.

It was not surprising that Edge and others understood so little about the airplane in 1910. One reason was that there was lots of experimentation with other forms of flight that at the time seemed to hold possibilities. Pilots flew balloons, dirigibles, and winged contraptions resembling hang gliders, but all lacked reliable systems of control. The pilot could not take the craft specifically where he wanted to go. Wilbur Wright had solved the control problem when, in a moment of inspiration, he had come up with wing-warping, or twisting the cloth-covered wings of his airplane via a system of wires. This twist of the wings gave the pilot control that had been unknown in other types of aircraft, allowing him to bank and maneuver with grace and with precision. The Wright brothers patented the wing-warping process.[39] Wing-warping evolved into ailerons—those flaps that raise and lower on airplane wings—and ailerons are still controlling airplanes.

At the start of their career in the sky, the brothers had discussed their work before other scientists and allowed would-be flyers to view their

experiments. Once wing-warping was found to be the key element in the
control of the airplane, others who were working on the concept of powered
flight immediately tried to imitate it. The Wrights responded by clamming
up and keeping their machine under wraps until their pending patents on
wing-warping and other facets of their airplane were granted. Without
much regard to the frustrations of a fascinated public, the brothers ignored
inquiries from disappointed reporters and the curious as they went about
improving the airplane and trying to sell it privately to various governments.
Their patent-related secrecy did not sit well with the press or the public.
After all, it had been widely told that Samuel Pierpont Langley, the secretary
of the Smithsonian Institution and a rival of the Wrights in developing
the airplane, would not claim a patent on the airplane when he invented
it. As one 1899 report had put it, "There will be no patents. There will be
no barriers to the genius of the world preventing investigation and further
improvement. This much Professor Langley has promised."[40] Of course,
the Wrights eventually beat him to the inventing punch, with Langley's
"Great Aerodrome" airplane crashing dramatically into the Potomac River
in Washington, D.C., a few days before the Wrights' successful first flight
at Kitty Hawk in 1903.[41] It would have been tacky of Langley to obtain a
patent on the Great Aerodrome, even if it had worked, since he had used
thousands of dollars in public money to build the doomed airplane.[42] Given
Langley's well-publicized failures and many stories of other failed flying
machines, the Wright brothers' secrecy didn't improve people's concepts
about aviation in general. Many thought the Wright brothers' claims of
flight were just so much bluster.[43]

   *Scientific American*, for one, was peeved by the Wrights' cloak and dagger
attitude. In May 1908, the magazine published a drawing of the Wright
Flyer in the air. Accompanying it was the following complaint:

   Upon the return of the newspaper correspondents and photographers from North Carolina [where the Wrights were experimenting],
   considerably more information was obtainable regarding the recent
   flights made by the Wright brothers in testing their aeroplane than
   has hitherto been available. Unfortunately, not one of these men is a

qualified technical observer, for which reason we are little better off for details than we were before.[44]

The magazine also ran two very distant photos of the Wright airplane in flight, grousing that the images were quite small, "but their greatest value lies in dispelling all doubt as to the ability of the Wright machine to fly and to make good its designers' claims."[45] Clearly *Scientific American* had been skeptical at best, and it was none too happy with the Wrights' lack of concern for their press relations. Meanwhile, *Scientific American* was much happier with flyer Glenn Curtiss, another Wright competitor. The magazine reported on Curtiss's first flight of May 22, 1908, in the Aerial Experiment Association's "White Wing" airplane, which the publication was allowed to photograph and describe.[46]

After the Wrights' patents on the airplane were granted, all would-be airplane builders were forced to redesign their aircraft radically to avoid Wright innovations. If flyers couldn't figure out a redesign, they had to obtain licenses from the Wrights or ply their trade in Europe, where American patent fights did not cause much worry. Either pilots took one of those options, or they faced a lawsuit from the Wrights. Orville wrote to Curtiss, "I learn from the *Scientific American* that your June Bug has movable surfaces at the tips of the wings, adjustable to different angles on the right and left side for lateral balance"—in other words, wing-warping. Here Orville referred Curtiss to the Wrights' U.S. Patent No. 831,393 and noted they had not given Curtiss nor his entourage "permission to use the patented features of our machine for exhibitions or in a commercial way." Orville made note, in the letter, of the basic truth that so grated with much of the public and press who wondered how one pair of brothers could get away with controlling all airplanes via one patent: "We believe it will be very difficult to develop a successful [flying] machine without the use of some of the features covered in this patent. If it is your desire to enter the exhibition business, we would be glad to take up the matter of a license to operate under our patents for that purpose."[47] Likewise, Louis Paulhan, the Frenchman who had starred in the Los Angeles air meet, discovered his airplane had been impounded because it infringed on Wright patents. Wilbur suggested Paulhan could get his airplane back by removing its vertical rudder, thus avoiding the patent conflict. Paulhan wisely refused to do so and simply quit flying in the United States for a while.[48]

The Wrights at first granted licenses to other flyers on an airplane-by-airplane basis. As time evolved, the inventors would license all airplanes in entire air shows, the licensing fee covering patent infringements.[49] But in early 1910, shortly after the Los Angeles meet ended, no one else was licensed, and non-Wright airplanes were all legally grounded in the United States. One of the darlings of the Los Angeles air meet, Curtiss, left the meet and headed straight to court to answer a charge of having violated Wright patents.[50] Aviator McGill at Mardi Gras claimed his airplane was an "improvement" over Wright Flyers[51]—that is, it was different enough to avoid patent infringement cases. No doubt, however, it actually used the Wrights' patented technology.

In early 1910, the only two airplanes in the United States legally operating were Wright airplanes flying in San Antonio, Texas, and Montgomery, Alabama.[52] Indeed, due to their long history of secrecy, the Wright brothers' battles against people who had violated their patents were far more widely known and understood than their airplane was.

At long last, in August 1908, *Scientific American* caught a great photo of Wilbur in flight at LeMans, France, after the Wright brothers came out of their cloistered existence to proclaim the perfection of flight to the world. At last the magazine was won over—if not a little miffed about not being given the story from the start. "We are glad to be able to present to our readers, in this issue, the first actual detail photographs of this world-renowned aeroplane which the Wright brothers have heretofore kept closely veiled from public view," the magazine said. "The Wright machine has demonstrated that it can fly in a wind as great as twenty miles an hour, while none of the other aeroplanes [designed by competitors of the Wrights] have ever flown in a wind of half this velocity. In this one point alone it is far superior to all other aeroplanes."[53]

Such interest by the scientific community fueled a frenzy of public interest in aviation, now often being reported by the Associated Press and finding its way into the popular imagination. Aviation was on everyone's mind, and since the notions of aviation were so very vague, almost any-thing passed as legitimate. Man was no longer earthbound. The sky was no longer the limit.

The reportorial department of the *Montgomery Advertiser* was swept up in aviation mania as well. In February 1910, an *Advertiser* reporter spoke with a Birmingham huckster, who fooled the writer into thinking he had built and been secretly flying an airplane around the north Alabama city at night. "His description of the sensations he suffered during his first flight seem so real, and what one would imagine they would be, that really there is little room to doubt him," the unnamed reporter said, justifying the story. "The inventor is a simple mechanic, not illiterate, but a man who hardly would be one to invent the sort of story he told from the imagination."[54]

However, the simple mechanic spun quite a yarn. He claimed that he was adapting Wright airplane designs in his own garage and that he was also constructing a passenger car for his airplane—a new idea in aviation. At the time, the pilot and one passenger sat on open seats mid-wing. The newfangled car being touted by the Birmingham inventor was constructed of fine French airplane cloth, coated with rubber. The car would carry four people, and its inventor assured the reporter that it would soon be photographed in flight to prove that he had invented a true passenger airplane.[55]

The pilot in the story, depicted as a self-taught mechanical genius (not unlike the popular—and accurate—image of the Wright brothers), had run into a very big snag at first. As he attempted his first flight, he became hideously airsick. His friends and witnesses "to their utter surprise found him [after the flight] lying flat on his back, bathed in perspiration and pale as death. He had come down just in time, for nausea had seized him and he was as limp as a rag, 'caring not whether he lived or died.'" The aviator had recovered enough, however, to be planning to begin flying passengers between Alabama and Washington, D.C., starting in a couple of months.[56] Such a huge distance of some 740 miles had never been tried by airplane before—200 miles was considered unthinkably far out of range.[57] Neverthe-less, the man calculated that the trip to Washington could be completed in thirty hours with four people in the airplane. "I'm going to do it long before the present session of Congress adjourns, informing the members of the august body of the time of my arrival by the wire so they may be on the lookout for me," he said. So far only a few friends knew the inventor's identity and could swear to the reporter that he was telling the truth—never mind that he had supposedly flown over the Birmingham suburb of Woodlawn in flights of more than an hour, and the pilot claimed that the residents there had seen him.[58]

Not surprisingly, no such pilot, airplane, or flights have ever come to light. But the reporter swallowed the whole story—and well he might, as E. T. Odum had constructed an airplane that he displayed at the state fair-

UP IN THE AIR.

**Advertiser *cartoonist Gilbert Edge used airplanes to depict the gubernatorial race.***

grounds in Birmingham a year earlier.[59] According to Odum, it was the only airplane that had been built in Birmingham. "I feel that I am on the right track and the only trouble now is to get a sufficiently powerful engine," he said, adding that he had actually gotten two wheels off the ground in one attempted flight.[60] The reporter may also have heard of Mobile resident John Fowler's unsuccessful huge-winged flying machine, constructed shortly after the first burst of aviation mania after the Wrights flew in 1903.[61] The *Advertiser*'s writer might even have known of Dr. Lewis Archer Boswell, who supposedly had invented and flown an airplane on his plantation in Eastaboga, Alabama, in 1894. Dr. Boswell had died in 1909, and if the unlikely claim was true, his secret died with him.[62] The lack of success of these home-built aircraft made reports of working aircraft all the more exciting.

The link of aviation and the future was powerful in the public psyche. The airplane was the symbol of progress. During the state's gubernatorial campaign, *Advertiser* cartoonist Edge portrayed five candidates flying about in Wright-style biplanes as they jockeyed for leadership. Unfortunately, the wings, as Edge drew them, were noticeably too short to support an airplane. While Edge may not have known how to draw a realistic airplane, he did have a sense of humor, suggesting in a pun in the cartoon that the outcome of the election was "up in the air."[63] While gubernatorial candidates debated the future, ordinary people in 1910 were struggling under staggering food costs and a rising cost of living. In a cartoon aptly entitled "Soaring," Edge portrayed the "Food Trust" as a grossly obese man flying a biplane. "I enjoy this immensely," the fat man said through his cigar, as he passed a falling hot air balloon sporting an empty food basket. Edge was knowledgeable enough of airplanes to realize that they were replacing balloons as the preferred air transport, but he had drawn no elevators or rudders to guide the Food Trust biplane, which featured wings that curved up in an unairworthy arc. Had the heavy pilot's airplane actually been able to get off the ground, it would have broken its propeller on landing, as the propeller was slung far below the undercarriage in Edge's unwittingly flawed drawing.[64]

Stretching aviation mania to its furthest imaginable point, W. Stewart Duncan wrote a long, sober feature in the *Advertiser* about the possibility of life on Mars. The feature quoted eminent scientists and took as a solid

SOARING

*Gilbert Edge's airplane-themed cartoon decrying the soaring cost of food.*

fact that the strange lines visible on the Martian surface were canals built by intelligent beings. Scientists were sure the Martians were melting their polar ice caps to cultivate vegetation, which experts said was clearly discernable. Some Earthlings were disappointed, however, that evolutionary logic precluded humans from being on Mars, there being no seas from which the evolution of the backbone could arise. Consequently, it seemed likely that the intelligent beings on Mars were antlike, with exoskeletons, Duncan said.[65] The inquiry into Martian life forms did not specifically mention aviation, and certainly men had long dreamed to know more of Mars. But the birth of aviation no doubt boosted discussion of fellow beings in space. Now that man was not entirely earthbound, the possibilities were dazzling!

Thus, Edge's choice of an airplane to depict the buoyant hope of the Montgomery and all-South publicity campaign was a good one. As the misdrawn airplane bobbed in the cartoon's night sky, casting a beam of light to the state below, neither Edge nor the *Advertiser*'s readers realized that the picture was extraordinarily prophetic. Quite unexpectedly, Montgomery was about to become the center of aviation in the United States. Publicity would come to Montgomery via the Wright brothers, and the world's foremost scientists would admire the city's electric streetcars and train system, which would bring thousands to see the local airplane in flight. Before the Wrights' students left town, indeed, the nation's first true night flights would be accomplished over the outskirts of Montgomery.

But in February of 1910, as Edge penned his cartoon biplanes, these twists of fortune were as yet unknown, and for that matter, Edge and his readers thought his depictions of airplanes were right on the money.

# 2

# THE SCHOOL IS FOUNDED

O n February 15, 1910, Wilbur Wright himself unexpectedly
showed up in Montgomery. Wilbur's arrival was an incredible
stroke of luck for Montgomery's soul-searching attempt to cast
itself as a place of opportunity, for he was searching for a place to start a
flying school. Like the Northern Mardi Gras revelers who had been lured
by the Progressive Union's publicity about balmy Southern winters, Wilbur
was hoping to find warmer temperatures and gentler winds than prevailed
in snowy Dayton, Ohio, where the Wright airplane company was based.
"He left Ohio some days ago on a trip through the South, going as far as
Jacksonville. There he was told of the wonderful climate of Central Alabama
and the great level and treeless areas of the Black Belt near Montgomery,"
the *Montgomery Advertiser* crowed, bursting with civic pride. "He took the
next train for the Capital City and has found what he wanted."[66]

Fred S. Ball, president of the Commercial Club of Montgomery (fore-
runner of the Chamber of Commerce), was the hero who discovered that
Wilbur was in town. Ball, a dapper attorney of forty-four, was passing
through the reading room of the club when he saw a bald, clean-shaven man
with chiseled features who looked so much like photographs of the famous
Wilbur Wright that Ball asked to be introduced. Indeed, it *was* Wilbur.
Ball put aside all personal business for the moment. "I was on my way to
try a case in court but stopped to talk with Mr. Wright," he recalled later.
"He had already visited Augusta and Atlanta, Ga., making investigations
of atmospheric and meteorological conditions, as well as landing facilities."
Ball hastily appointed a committee of leading men in the Commercial Club

to take advantage of the windfall by working with Wilbur.[67]

As it turned out, it took a lot of work on the part of the prominent Montgomerians to see that forty-two-year-old Wilbur found what he wanted. One factor—the weather—they could not control, but luckily the famous inventor was already charmed by that aspect of Montgomery. The winds suited him. As he noted in his diary, winds in Montgomery were "not over 4–5 miles at any time"[68]—ideal for teaching young pilots. But as the city's businessmen realized, there was much more to be accomplished for the sake of the Wizard of the Air than just having ideal wind conditions. They had already been thinking about luring that Army post, so they had a sense of what type of action had to be undertaken. Prominent members of the Commercial Club wasted no time in inviting Wilbur to lunch with them at the Exchange Hotel to discuss what he would need.[69] As they found out, he was searching for a level, tree-free field on which to teach a schoolful of pilots.

Commercial Club Secretary Mr. Hyman accordingly took Wilbur on

*Left, Wilbur Wright, whom Fred Ball recognized from having seen pictures such as this. Right, Ball, president of the Montgomery Commercial Club. His quick action helped get the Wright flying school off the ground.*

a motor car tour of the city, showing him various sites that might make a good airfield. So great was the Commercial Club's desire to secure the Wright presence in Montgomery that club members considered sacrificing the golf links at the country club as an airfield. The hedges surrounding each hole were too much for young pilots, however; Wilbur worried that students would crash into them. The Club next thought that perhaps the city could do without its fairgrounds. But that land, Wilbur determined, was too uneven and too fenced in. He certainly could not set up student pilots to crash into fences. As Wilbur explained to his hosts, new pilots' worst habit was to land too quickly, and hedges and fences were thus magnets for disaster.[70]

As Mr. Hyman drove Wilbur through all the available or unavailable public lands, local powerhouses in the Commercial Club were checking private lands. Never mind that they didn't consult the various landowners first. They only hoped publicly via the press that the cost of the land would not be too high for the aviators—a none-too-subtle hint to any whose land might be so blessed as to be picked by Wilbur.[71]

As the whirlwind tour progressed, it seemed this idea of buying private property was the ticket. The *Advertiser* reported that Wilbur was "most pleased" with the Hunter Vaughan plantation. "A more ideal place could not be secured for this [aviation] work," the newspaper explained as much to Vaughan as to its readers. Vaughan was using a large part of the area for pasture anyway, and *surely* he could relinquish it for the Wright brothers, the newspaper suggested—although Vaughan himself had apparently not yet been asked his opinion on the matter. Adjoining the Vaughan property was land owned by F. B. Fisk, which Wilbur also liked. The lands under consideration were flat and fairly free of bushes and hedges. The paper reported excitedly, "Mr. Wright has practically decided to locate his training and experimental camp here for the spring and will do so if satisfactory business arrangements can be made."[72] Meanwhile, to hasten a positive decision, Ball got Montgomery's leading bankers and businessmen to send telegrams and letters promising aid to the Wrights to help convince Wilbur to alight permanently in Alabama.[73] It was just the kind of tactic the military expert had suggested might work to lure an Army base to the area.

There were irritations amidst all the excitement, however. The local press brought up some questions that the businessmen would rather have ignored. The *Advertiser* asked Wilbur about the popular perception that airplanes were a menace. Couldn't they be used by smugglers or other criminals? Wilbur laughed at that, pointing out, "There are too few [airplanes] in use for the authorities not to be able to keep track of them, and any smuggling done would readily be traced to them . . . Burglars attempting a descent on a city would be spotted at once as soon as a robbery was reported. There is no danger of flying machines ever being used by criminals." Likewise, the pioneer aviator scoffed at the fear that Count Zeppelin's dirigibles, currently the hot aviation item in Germany, would ever be used to invade England. Dirigibles, he explained, cost way too much—on average, $250,000 (more than thirty-three times the retail price of a Wright Flyer). "They are far too delicate for military work," he assured the newspaper. "They are wrecked almost every time they leave the sheds. A landing generally puts them out of business, and in the air and on the ground they are utterly at the mercy of a high wind."[74]

When pressed by the reporter, Wilbur also was forced to comment on the constant and unpleasant legal battles he and his company were fighting over patent infringements. Although his words belied the brothers' unending worries about patent infringement, Wilbur claimed that he was not afraid of copycats. Flying, he said, was too expensive for the amateur to figure out on his own. Men who had the means would just as soon buy one of the Wright Company airplanes now being manufactured for sale in Dayton, in Wilbur's opinion.[75]

After defending airplanes and boosting the Wright factory, Wilbur refused to say anything more. This was a huge disappointment to the *Advertiser*'s writer, who complained, "He firmly but pleasantly declined to discuss any of his wonderful adventures abroad, and is about the most reticent man a reporter ever went up against."[76] The reporter's frustration may have had something to do with his selection of just the right words to describe Wilbur to the celebrity-worshipping readership of the *Advertiser*. "Wilbur Wright," the reporter wrote in a backhanded compliment, "has been cruelly maligned by his published photographs. Judging from them he looks like he is in the last stages of some incessantly gnawing disease. In reality he is almost boyish looking, clear-skinned, bright-eyed, athletic and young."[77]

That gossipy kind of description had to do when Wilbur refused to give the press any real news. The press tried valiantly to find something to say about an untalkative but much-appreciated guest but continually had to resort to rather far-fetched filler. For example, the *Advertiser*'s reporter spent part of a story discussing the first case of heavier-than-air flight—that of Icarus in Greek mythology. He speculated as well as to how many men and airplanes Wilbur would bring to Montgomery. Most likely, he guessed, two or three airplanes would soon be flying overhead, and Wilbur would bring his own portable shed to house them. Unable to pin down how big Wilbur's "corps of aerial chauffeurs" would be, the writer did note that the pilots-in-training were needed for the new career of teaching buyers of airplanes how to fly them.[78]

The next day, the *Advertiser* was jubilant to report that its own news story had had a hand in securing the Wright brothers' presence in Montgomery. City businessman Frank Kohn had offered the Wrights use of his cotton plantation, free of charge, for an "aeroplane" camp. Kohn, a distinguished-looking real estate and insurance agent transplanted from Philadelphia, was known around town as a leader in the attempt to advance Montgomery. Kohn had read in the *Advertiser* that the only obstacle to securing the Wright brothers' training camp was the cost of land. He offered a three-mile-square tract of his plantation at no charge.[79] Kohn's land, just north and west of the city, included much of the community known as Douglasville, a village inhabited by black field hands who worked Kohn's cotton fields.[80] Wilbur visited the spot and immediately telegraphed orders to Dayton to pack up a Flyer and send it to Alabama, declaring the Kohn field to be one of the best flying fields he had ever seen.[81] The great airman said he expected both Orville and himself to run the flight school.[82]

The news was almost too good to be true—the city was all at once thrust into the aviation limelight that Edge had dreamed of in his editorial cartoon only fourteen days before! The forward-thinking men of the Commercial Club had to seize the moment. They sprang into action to create the kind of atmosphere that Montgomery would need if it wished to exploit the publicity that could and should arise from being the aviation capital of the nation. The fledgling aviation reporter at the *Advertiser* was poetic in his praise. "With public spirited energy, Frank D. Kohn cut the Gordian knot in the matter of [a] suitable training ground for the Wright aeroplane camp," the writer sang. "Having the city's best interest at heart, he did not consider that possible damage may be done his planted acres by the crowds that will go out to see the flying machine. All he could see was the best advertisement Montgomery has ever had."[83]

All of the businessmen in the Commercial Club, not just Kohn, rolled out the red carpet for the Wright brothers with the thought that their presence could only bring positive publicity to Montgomery. The longer the famous flyers stayed in town, the better for the city. Commercial Club members intended to keep the Wright brothers from spending a penny of their own money, a key element in the project to lure the Wrights to Alabama permanently. Already the businessmen were scheming to find donated automobiles for the famous brothers' use in getting to the airfield, and word around town was that any lumber company that donated materials for

*Frank D. Kohn, businessman, cotton grower, and Montgomery booster. He sacrificed some of his cotton acreage for the Wright school.*

the hangar would benefit by a lot of free publicity as a Wright benefactor. Secretary Hyman of the Commercial Club got Wilbur to describe exactly the building he wanted—forty-five feet long by thirty-six feet deep by ten feet high. The front was to feature sliding or folding doors, with the entire building made of tongue-and-groove boards caulked to keep the rain out. Hyman took charge of the construction project, declaring optimistically that work would begin and end within the week.[84]

The thought that Montgomery, not to mention area businesses, would gain a publicity boon by the Wright presence was not far-fetched. Thirty telegrams had already come to Wilbur from other Southern cities, making all-expenses-paid pledges and offering monetary bonuses in an attempt to entice the Wright school away from Montgomery. In a worried bid to turn Wilbur away from any flirtations by other cities, Hyman took Wilbur to the local Weather Bureau. The records there showed that Montgomery had half the rainfall of Atlanta, Nashville, and Memphis, and Montgomery could brag of an average wind velocity of just seven miles per hour. Those things, too, pleased Wilbur, and those were things that other places could not match.[85]

"The press of the world will watch his work in this city," the *Advertiser* said soberly, ". . . and stories about Montgomery and about Central Alabama will be in every paper in every town which The Associated Press reaches." Montgomery truly had a chance to put itself prominently on America's map as an aviation center—with lots of other good things about the city to be made known across the nation.[86]

If boosting Montgomery was the central theme of the developing drama, however, Wilbur Wright was not too clear about his role in the script. That second day in town, he announced, "We are here for work," and he explained that he would take no passengers during the duration of the training camp. He momentarily let down his guard to tell an interesting story that explained his position regarding passengers:

> Now about this thing of taking up people. It's out of the line of the present work. We have a great deal of work to do and know that we will be retarded somewhat by visitors. Of course, we will allow people to come and see what is going on, if they want to, but will not take passengers up. I remember, while taking lunch with the King of Spain, he said he wanted me to take up one of his officers. There was nothing for me to do but say "Yes," but I knew the officer in question and did not want him to go with me. But we went out to the aviation field that evening, and made ready. I took my place in the machine

and—but I forgot, I am talking to a newspaper man. I have to make
ready for the train now, good-bye.[87]

It was a brush-off in vintage Wright fashion—the brothers had never
much worried about their public image. Wilbur had a job to do, and that
was that. The reporter, however, did not take the brush-off kindly. "Appeals
and cajolery had no effect, Wilbur Wright had closed like a cotton compress.
There was nothing more to be secured from him, and what became of the
Spanish officer is not recorded history," the reporter snapped.[88]

A peculiar battle had just been fought in the publicity war, and Montgomery had come out of it with its plans badly wounded. Wilbur was the
much-needed general in the war for the progress of Alabama, but he had
certainly not taken command in the way Montgomerians had hoped.

The *Advertiser* and civic-minded men of Montgomery didn't give much
regard to Wilbur's desire for privacy. A good public relations image was critical
for Montgomery, if it were going to be on front pages around the nation.
Commercial Club Secretary Hyman predicted that more than 100,000
visitors would likely go to the Kohn plantation to see the brothers in the
next two months[89]—and the city had only 78,000 residents. Hyman told
the *Advertiser* that visitors would come not just from Alabama or the South,
but from throughout the United States—much as the Progressive Union
had expected visitors from all over the place to come see the Mardi Gras airships. Although people likely would have shown up to see the Montgomery
airplane without such an estimate by the local press, Hyman's statements
in the newspaper amounted to a thinly veiled invitation to anyone who
wondered if spectators were welcome at the aviation camp.

Apropos of the Commercial Club's goal for the city in its sudden new
involvement with aviation, the *Advertiser* reported Hyman's assessment
that "the advent of Montgomery into the flying machine circle will have an
advertising value almost equivalent to an exposition." Of course, a world-
class exposition in a small city like Montgomery was unheard of, so this
worldwide attention was an unmistakable windfall. "The value of the coming
of the Wrights has struck the Montgomery business men in the right place
and already leading houses have proffered money and goods free of all cost,"

the *Advertiser* reported. John P. Kohn (brother of the landowner, Frank) offered to build the "aerie," as the newspaper called the airplane's hangar, but his offer was hardly necessary, given that some twenty businessmen had already stepped forward to contribute to the cost of the project. An architect drew plans for the aerie just one day after the specifications were given, and Hyman put them in the mail to Dayton.[90]

Now all of the businessmen's boasting and speculating about support of the brothers had to come true. Hyman summoned automobile dealers and notified them that they would need to supply a car for the Wright brothers, and the *Advertiser* put public pressure on the dealers by an-nouncing that it fully expected one of these businesses to donate a car. The newspaper sweetened the deal by noting that the donation would amount to some great advertisement for the dealership. But there *was* a "Plan B"— if no goodhearted auto dealer stepped forward to donate a car, then local men had already planned to alternate the loan of their automobiles to the Wrights.[91] Indeed, such elaborate covering of all bases was necessary, for the Commercial Club had promised in its original bargain with Wilbur that it would furnish transportation for him and his students to and from their lodgings in Montgomery.[92]

The excitement among Montgomerians did not stop with the issue of transporting the inventors of the airplane. Whole careers might begin with the Wright camp. "Guards will be needed to keep the crowds in order," the *Advertiser* explained, adding, "These men will probably be commissioned as deputies by the county authorities." Night watchmen would also be hired, "and, of course," the newspaper speculated in a completely unfounded (and, as it turned out, inaccurate) guess, "there is the possibility of several daring local boys securing positions among the men who are to be trained in sky navigation."[93]

The Commercial Club at least paid lip service to Wilbur's desire for privacy. Wilbur's Commercial Club sponsors talked with him about the public's desire to see the airplane, and Wilbur promised to set aside certain days for visitors, when "every courtesy" would be shown to them. For its part, the Commercial Club would see to it that Wilbur would be allowed to do his work on non-spectator days, and the club would also take on the responsibility of keeping the field under guard. Perhaps to handle the disappointment of spectators who would not be allowed in the aviation camp on ordinary training days, the *Advertiser* repeated Wilbur's assertion that students' flights would be low and unspectacular, due to the pilots' novice status and the critical need to practice landings. On visiting days, however, the Wrights themselves would do "the most interesting [flying] of all."[94]

There was an ugly side to all the upbeat coverage. The *Advertiser*'s editor, curmudgeonly old William Wallace Screws, was hostile toward aviation in general and the Wrights in particular. Now in the twilight of a journalism career that had begun in the Civil War, Screws had long played a critical role in getting Democrats elected to office. He was a powerful voice in Alabama and relished the role. At age seventy-one, he had mixed feelings about the viability of newfangled aviation.[95] He did not have mixed feelings about Orville Wright, however, who was often unpopular with members of the press. Screws showcased an Associated Press story that described Orville as "taciturn" and uncooperative. The article complained that Orville's "public utterances thus far chronicled are summed up largely in the phrases 'It's too windy,' 'I thank you,' and the like." This time, however, the younger of the brothers had finally opened up to the press to speak disparagingly about Frenchmen's attempt to evade trouble over copying Wright patents, and the story focused on that. A decision to stage an aviation meet in France to avoid Wright patent litigation in the United States caused Orville to say of the French, "It is characteristic of the race. When they are defeated in anything they do not come back next time with an attempt to regain a lost cup. They organize a new meet and get a new cup for which they competed on their own grounds." The article was clearly unflattering to Orville, even in 1910 before ethnic prejudice was considered unenlightened. The Associated Press went on to quote Orville as deriding airplanes that had been stripped of mechanisms that violated Wright patents. "So will an automobile go a short way without any hand upon the steering gear," he sneered, "but it will not go far."[96]

Yet Montgomery loved Wilbur. His brother may have looked like a fool to the Associated Press, but Wilbur himself was giving Montgomery the boost it craved. The article that criticized Orville went on to brag that

Montgomery had been picked by Wilbur over Augusta, Georgia, and that the mild, dry temperatures of Montgomery were a bonus to the famous aviators. The *Advertiser* also announced joyfully that the Wrights would actually set up a manufacturing plant to produce airplanes in Montgomery,[97] a report that turned out to be wishful thinking.

Gilbert Edge, the *Advertiser's* editorial cartoonist, in keeping with his recent cartoon on airplanes and Montgomery publicity, eagerly exploited the Wilbur bonanza. On February 24, the artist drew a cartoon showing Wilbur and a lovely "Miss Montgomery" flying above the city in a biplane—never mind Wilbur's assertion that he would not take up passengers. Perhaps by now having studied up on the matter, Edge avoided drawing another faulty biplane by focusing tightly on Wilbur and his comely guest and thus not having to draw the wings at all. "We're pleased to have you with u[s] Mr. Wright," the lady said, while an eagle representing America—sitting atop the plane and dressed in a jaunty Uncle Sam hat—said, "I've got my eyes on both of you." Characteristically, the great aviator said nothing.[98]

Meanwhile, Montgomery needed to build that aerie. On March 1, a few days after he left Montgomery for Ohio, Wilbur sent Fred Ball and the Commercial Club a telegram, explaining that he was ready to pack up the airplane and move from Dayton to Montgomery as soon as the hangar was constructed. Ball hastily notified contractors to meet him the next morning on the Kohn plantation, which was three miles from the city. Landowner Frank Kohn was one of the men tapped to select an appropriate site for the building.[99]

Usually the erecting of a small building wouldn't merit much press attention, but a small building for the Wizard of the Air—well, that was a different matter altogether. When he had last been in town, Wilbur had doubted the businessmen's well-meaning plan to get the aerie built in a week. The record for fast shed-building, Wilbur had said at the time, belonged to him, when he built his own first shed. Then he had issued what everyone took to be a challenge. "The next best [time in shed-building] was that built at [Pau, France]. King Alfonso, of Spain, was back of that and he saw to it that the work was quickly done," Wilbur had said. "I think fifty Spanish carpenters were at work on the little building."[100]

WITH WRIGHT

*Wilbur Wright said he would not take up passengers, but cartoonist Gilbert Edge couldn't resist depicting "Miss Montgomery" along for the ride. All of America, symbolized by the eagle, watched both "Miss Montgomery" and Wilbur.*

Could Montgomerians trump the very king of Spain? It would not be easy to produce the high quality that Wilbur demanded in the short time that he preferred. "The utmost care is to be observed in the construction of the shed. The building is to house a very valuable piece of mechanism and no chances will be taken with poor construction," the *Advertiser*'s budding aviation reporter explained on Wednesday, March 2. "The best materials and best workmanship available will be utilized in the work and it will be ready for Mr. Wright's use by next Monday."[101] It was hard to reckon how the site for a high-quality building could be selected on Wednesday and the building finished on Monday, but Montgomery businessmen were determined to try.

Hard information on the nonexistent aerie was scarce, so the *Advertiser* published nonexistent information in its place. "Before leaving Montgomery, three weeks ago, Mr. Wright said he would have a flying machine packed and shipped to Montgomery as soon as he reached Dayton," the newspaper said. Then it went on to paint a very imaginative scene: "It is believed that the boxes containing the parts of the machine have already reached the city and are being guarded carefully by the railroad over which the shipment was made."[102] In reality, the machine wouldn't arrive at the ornate and modern Union Station for two more weeks.[103] The newspaper announced that the airplane would be in the air by the second week of March,[104] when in reality the airplane wouldn't get off the ground until the last week of the month.[105] Just as speculatively, the newspaper said with authority rooted entirely in guesswork (and inaccurate guesswork at that) that Wilbur would return to Montgomery that week to oversee construction of the aerie. His presence would save valuable time in construction, the newspaper explained. In another burst of imagination, the newspaper reported that the Kohn plantation was strongly fenced to keep away curiosity seekers, and that mounted guards might be on hand "to keep order," making the field sound just short of a prison camp. However, as the newspaper explained once again, the field must stay clear while training was in progress. Crowds would simply not be allowed except on visiting days, as Commercial Club President Ball reiterated for the press. In fact, the newspaper quoted Wilbur himself, suggesting he had said before he left Montgomery that "he was quite willing for those who had never seen an aeroplane to get at least one view of the machine, but he also said he was here for business, and this would be the first consideration always."[106]

That limitation being the case, people who lived near the airfield were sprucing up their houses so that they could charge others for the chance to watch the airplane from their property. Not only that, but some of Montgomery's skyscrapers might offer a chance to see the airplane—for a fee, of course.[107] The two-year-old skyscraper owned by N. J. Bell featured 871 windows and even a roof garden. Surely the airplane would be visible there, as it might also be from the equally tall First National Bank building. That 1896 terra cotta-clad skyscraper seemed to be staring toward the Kohn place, anyway; it featured decorative lion heads looking out in all directions around the roofline.[108] Lucky owners of such venues stood to make a "pretty penny," as the *Advertiser* explained things.[109] Later, however, the newspaper admitted that viewers in the Bell building and First National Bank, both towering twelve stories, would only be able to see the airplane by using binoculars, "but there are many houses on the edge of town that also command a view of the field."[110]

Enthusiastic Montgomerians, eager to make a fine showing for the city, pitched in to make the Wright camp a reality. Contractor D. F. Gorrie arrived on the scene on Thursday, March 3, and said he could indeed have the aerie ready by noon on the following Monday, March 7. The Commercial Club, meanwhile, called a special meeting to work out the specifics of how the united businessmen of Montgomery would foot the bills for the Wrights, as they had planned to do.[111]

The Wright project grew more and more appealing. The Wright machine in Montgomery would be the only airplane in operation in North America. Patent lawsuits were keeping all Wright imitators from flying, and the only other authorized Wright airplane in the nation was the U.S. government's model, then being flown for military use in San Antonio, Texas. That machine had recently been damaged in a crash, leaving the Montgomery airplane the only one in the air. In fact, the Associated Press calculated that only three men in the world, besides the Wrights themselves, knew how to pilot the Wright airplane.[112] The estimate of three men in the entire world was too low, but it was roughly accurate for the United States. Those three American pilots were very fresh at their jobs, too—Wilbur had just finished training the three Army pilots who were assigned to fly the new military airplane in San Antonio.[113] "This situation in flying machine circles will draw the eyes of those in the country interested in aerial navigation to Montgomery, for here only will they be able to get news of flying machine development," the *Advertiser* explained.[114] Even editor Screws got caught up in the spirit. He commented:

> The Wright Brothers, the acknowledged inventors of flying machines, saw their opportunity and seized it. They realized that Montgomery, with its central location, its splendid climate and its easy access, furnished an ideal site for the building of their "aerie"—a place for the demonstration of flying machines. The coming of the Wrights will be a benefit both to them and to the city of Montgomery.
>
> Other aviators may claim in the courts . . . that their flying machines were not built on the Wright idea and that there has been no infringement on the Wright [patents] and inventions. But the cold and indisputable fact remains that after centuries of vain effort no man ever made a heavier than air machine that flew until the Wright boys, after years of untiring efforts, found the secret and launched a machine that took the air and glided like a bird over the sands of a land locked bay.
>
> When descriptions of the machine had been published imitators of the Wrights sprung up in Europe and America. There are many flying machines but there was none until the Wright Brothers solved the problem.
>
> Their place in history is secure.[115]

Screws couldn't resist an extra plug for Montgomery: "Undoubtedly our excellent climate contributed largely in persuading the aviators to select Montgomery as their training ground. In working for our commercial development we should urge the patent fact that the climate of Middle Alabama is second to none in the world."[116]

Meanwhile, construction of the aerie had passed the deadline but was racing forward. After the Monday, March 7, target date came and went, Fred Ball announced that the aerie would be finished by the night of Wednesday the ninth, when the doors would be hung and the roof would be tarred.[117] He turned out to be correct. When the aerie was completed Wednesday afternoon, Secretary Hyman of the Commercial Club nailed a big United States flag on a gilded pole to the aerie roof.[118]

The field itself was cleared of a few trees[119] and some undergrowth, and it appeared that the treeless section of the Kohn plantation was really a flying field—if only the pilots and airplane would turn up.[120] Speculation still ran high that the Wrights had already sent their airplane, now under guard, and that flights would start by week's end. "The expectant Alabama public will soon be given the treat for which it has been longing," the *Advertiser* promised.[121]

Other progress was—hopefully—afoot. The *Advertiser* declared that the embarrassingly inadequate Washington Ferry Road that led to the camp ought to be fixed up, noting that "although not exactly in bad condition, it is hardly a sample of Montgomery county good roads." The Commercial Club, in fact, intended to pressure county and city authorities on the matter. After all, thousands of people would be traveling that way to see the airplane in action. "[The road] is not much more than a hundred yards long and a few dollars and a few days work would put it in first class condition," the club reasoned. If an aerie could be built in less than a week, why couldn't a road be fixed up overnight? The *Advertiser* thought that electric lights around the camp would be in order as well, certainly matching up to Montgomery's place in electrification history.[122]

Those ideas for improvements became urgent when a telegram arrived from F. H. Russell of the Wright Company with the welcome news that the airplane was ready to ship and would be sent in the next few days.[123] "Its arrival and that of the aviators are all that remain to make Montgomery the flying machine center of the United States," the *Advertiser* exulted.[124] In fact, the entire *world* would focus its attention on Montgomery, courtesy of the Wrights, the *Advertiser* predicted.[125]

As soon as the airplane arrived via special car on the Louisville and

Nashville Railroad in seven boxes, along with a boxcar of material that the aviators would use, the excitement increased to a gloriously concrete level. The airplane parts were actually *there*. The aviation writer for the *Advertiser* reported on March 16 that the assorted materials included special lumber, wire, steel, canvas, and radiators—all unloaded while the breathless reporter looked on. Guesswork was still the rule, however, for the rest of the story. No one had as yet heard from Wilbur, so the reporter speculated that he would bring six United States Army officers with him, to instruct them in flying. The officers, the self-styled expert writer said, would be allowed to fly only ten feet from the ground until they got used to the airplane.[126] Two days later the writer admitted that no one really knew when the men would arrive.[127] It was pretty hard to keep a story alive when nothing much was happening.

One thing that did seem to be happening was that many visitors were already going out to see the hangar. The *Advertiser* worked this out, Sherlock Holmes-fashion, by noting that the "well beaten surface of this road already indicates the presence of many visitors at the camp." And although Wilbur had asked to be left alone, that request was falling by the wayside before he even returned. The Southern Railroad was contemplating putting on a shuttle train from the city to the field[128] (reminiscent of the Progressive Union's train tickets to Mardi Gras), even though the only thing to see at the moment on the Montgomery flying field was the aerie, which was covered with local advertisements.

"Montgomery merchants were quick to see the advertising value of the selection by the Wrights of this city for spring headquarters," the *Advertiser* commented in a dry understatement.[129] The firm of Webber & Johnston, for example, had lettered a large sign on the front exterior wall of the hangar, which read, "Our Prices, Like 'Wilbur,' are 'Wright,' but they are not 'up in the air.'" That was just one of several companies that used the building as a giant billboard. D. F. Gorrie & Son, the construction company, announced proudly on the building that it had put up the shed in just three days. "This building was covered by Montgomery Roofing & Cornice Co.," announced the roofers, noting that they had architectural sheet metal for sale, not to mention cornices, copper roofs, and workers to install them.

*Montgomery merchants contributed to the fast-built airplane shed for commercial reasons, at least in part. The "aerie" was a giant billboard hawking various local products.*

Vesuvius Lumber Company used the shed to announce it could furnish building materials of all kinds, while Sol Cadden proclaimed that he was a leading purveyor of clothes and furnishings. Another sign bragged about a type of "Coffee Making Montgomery Famous"—the St. Regis Special. The ad implored onlookers to "ask your grocer about it." There were still other advertising signs on the doors, and some on the roof, including a rooftop ad for biscuits. Interestingly, the rooftop ads were legible mostly to the aviators—the pilots were perhaps the only people high enough to read them clearly.[130]

In exchange for touting their wares in the Wrights' private domain, the merchants had by now worked out exactly how they would supply the brothers' needs free of cost. "Montgomery business men say they will make the Wrights' visit so profitable as well as pleasant that the aviators will wish to make the training camp a permanent institution," an *Advertiser* report stated rather hopefully.[131]

Businesses took advantage of aviation mania as it swept through town. One, local department store Montgomery Fair, itself fit the new, progressive image symbolized by the Wright Flyer. The massive, four-story building had its roots in old Montgomery, where it had started as Pollak's Dollar Store in 1868. By 1898 it was called "The Fair," and now, its expanded name "Montgomery Fair" seemed to boast of the city's newfound downtown beauty as much as it bragged about the wide array of toiletries, neckties, corsets, linens, toys, clothing, cloth, and other goods you could buy there. In fact, the store, which claimed to be one of the largest in the South, had only recently opened a third entrance on Court Street.[132] Truly, the store was doing its part to modernize Montgomery. Embracing Montgomery's sudden aviation fortune, Montgomery Fair hastily ordered for sale Carter's Aeroplane No. 1, a ten- by twelve-inch toy it described as "a miniature air ship embodying most features of the larger machines." The toy airplane in fact looked nothing like the real thing, featuring an upwardly curved set of wings, a propeller on either end, and a weight suspended from the bottom. Not that even in-the-know readers would recognize it as an airplane anyway, for Montgomery Fair officials or the *Advertiser*'s compositors (or both) were so ignorant of airplanes that they first ran the picture of the toy sideways. Ignorance aside, the little airplane was certainly hawked with enthusiasm. Children, Montgomery Fair said, could fly the airplane for one hundred fifty feet, and the toy could be easily adjusted to fly right or left or up or down. "It is a novel and amusing device for use out of doors or in the house," the store said. The advertisement also bragged, "Montgomery has the honor of being the first city in the country to receive a shipment of these air ships." Apparently local children would have more interest than would children in any other town, Montgomery being the momentary capital of aviation. The toy could be had for twenty-five cents.[133]

Another company trying to capitalize on the Wright presence was the Southern Shoe Surgery, which invited the Wrights to tour its shop and then turned that fact into an ad in the *Advertiser*. The ad was made to look like an article with the enticing headline, "Wright Bros. Given Cordial Invitation." The ad reflected Montgomery's feelings about the Wrights' role in giving local businesses a shot in the arm. "As the citizens of Montgomery are very desirous of having the 'Wizards of the Air' see the commercial side of this city as well as the social, an invitation has been given to them to inspect the new plant of the Southern Shoe Surgery, 18 S. Perry St.," the ad

*Toy "Air Ships" could be had at Montgomery Fair Department Store for 25 cents. Airplanes were so unfamiliar, however, that the ad ran with the picture sideways on March 20 (left). By March 25 (right), the* Advertiser *realized its mistake.*

ran. "There they will see the Shoe Surgeons amputate old soles and replace them with whole new soles. All the customers have to do is call 1073 and the shoe ambulance will be sent after the shoes."[134]

When Wright associates Charles E. Taylor, James W. Davis, and Walter R. Brookins arrived at the camp on March 19, the city's excitement was nearing fever pitch. The newspaper learned from the men that the airplane the crew would now put together was the very one that Wilbur had flown around the Statue of Liberty and up the Hudson River during the 1909 Hudson-Fulton celebration, with thousands of New Yorkers witnessing the flight. Thus, the airplane itself was already a celebrity. Indeed, as the *New York Tribune* had sung in 1909, the famous statue had turned her crowned head to look at the airplane, a not-made-up fact, the paper had claimed, "because thousands of pairs of eyes" saw it happen. Wilbur, the New York report had warbled, showed "mankind how it might be liberated from the thraldom of earth."[135]

The *Advertiser*'s awestruck description of the significant New York flight made in 1909 by Montgomery's very own airplane gives an indication of how futuristic and incredible flight seemed to ordinary people of 1910. Apparently it was a privilege even to be allowed to gaze upon such a great airplane:

> Montgomerians will be permitted to see the same machine in which Wilbur Wright drew the plaudits of thousands last fall at the Hudson-Fulton celebration in New York. In this machine, the bold aviator dared wind and wave when he traveled up and down the Hudson, high above the masts of a great assemblage of fighting and merchant craft. And in the same aeroplane he astonished the onlookers by circling the great statue of the Goddess of Liberty in the harbor.[136]

Despite all the excitement of having a celebrity of an airplane in town, the Wright Company employees who accompanied the machine were unmoved by the fuss. Taylor, Davis, and Brookins duly congratulated their boss for selecting such a fine site for the training camp and went to work putting the aircraft together.[137] When it was done, it would weigh 800 pounds, or 902 pounds with its full load of gasoline and water, and 190 pounds of the total would be the motor. The four-cylinder motor would generate twenty-five to thirty-five horsepower. The wings, now being assembled, would be placed one atop another six feet apart. They were forty-one feet long and six and a half feet wide, and the pilot and student would sit in open seats on the lower wing. Sticking out ten feet behind would be two parallel vertical rudders, and ten feet to the front would be two parallel horizontal elevators. The airplane would also feature two "pusher" propellers mounted behind the wings. Focusing on what seemed the most important issue to him, however, the Commercial Club's Fred Ball noted with satisfaction that the Montgomery-built aerie was "amply large" for the purpose of building and storing such a large piece of machinery.[138]

# 3

# THE GREAT SPECTATOR SPORT

U nfortunately for the excited city of Montgomery, the arrival of the Wrights' crew did not immediately start the great spectator sport that the city had envisioned. The airmen seemed to be doing their best to squelch any cheering from the sidelines. They wanted to be left alone.

It was a tough blow, one that the city did not take well. The *Advertiser*'s reporter hurried to the aviation camp for interviews on March 19, and, as had happened with Wilbur, the workers at the camp snubbed him. Once again the newly styled aviation reporter sulked about it. "The work of assembling the aeroplane is in [the] charge of Mr. Taylor. He and his assistants, following the Wright policy, make confidants of none," the reporter grumbled. "Further than to declare that they had been detailed to Montgomery to construct the aeroplane, they were reticent. They would give no expression as to the probable date of the Wrights' arrival, nor of the beginning of active operations."[139]

The next day the story was the same. Under the main headline of the article, the subheading proclaimed, "Too Busy to Talk to Public. Questions Tabooed at Camp." The aviation writer complained, "A politely frigid stare will be the only reply given by the three attaches from the Dayton factory to any Montgomerians whose curiosity moves them to give expression to their inquisitiveness." The writer went on to quote Charles Taylor rather unflatteringly: "'Yes,' said Mr. Taylor Sunday night, 'visitors to the camp may ask all the questions they desire, but they must answer these themselves. We were sent here to get the aeroplane in readiness for Mr. Wright's coming, and we have not time to instruct the public concerning the various phases of our work.'" The reporter did add—rather hopefully—Taylor's comment that the public would be given "ample opportunity to see the aeroplane in action" when his boss arrived. After much pouting from spectators who had found the camp already, the Wright crew was forced to dodge the adulation by its instant and insistent fan club. As the *Advertiser* explained it, "To protect occasional visitors to the camp from feeling that they are being snubbed when questions remain unanswered, the Wright Company men have determined to enclose a certain space about the aeroplane shed by means of ropes. Inside these ropes the public will not be permitted to come."[140]

Despite the reporter's pique about the politely frigid stare, Charles Taylor did give him a decent interview. A long-time employee of the Wright brothers, Taylor had worked in the Wright shop as a mechanic from their days as bicycle merchants. It was he who had built the wind tunnel that enabled the Wrights to discover the proper shape of a wing in 1901. It was Taylor who had figured out how to build the lightweight motor that powered the first airplane—a feat he accomplished in six weeks in 1903, even though his entire prior knowledge of motors came from his one attempt to fix an automobile motor two years earlier.[141] Aside from the Wrights, he had seen more of the airplane than anyone in the world. Thus, it was no small praise when Taylor compared the Alabama training camp favorably to the U.S. War Department flying grounds at Fort Myer, Virginia. "Our training camp here is much better than at Fort Myer," Taylor said. "At Fort Myer, when an ascent was made, it was necessary to remain in the air until a return to the parade ground. The topography of the land prevented a descent outside this space, except in an emergency." But the Kohn plantation was far superior. "At this camp, this condition will not be encountered, for the broad stretch of flat country makes a descent easy and without much trouble in case it is desired," Taylor explained. Even better, takeoff would be more natural, he said. In Fort Myer, the space was so tight that Orville was forced to start the airplane on an incline and to increase takeoff speed with the use of weights which, when dropped from the top of a derrick-like device, helped catapult the airplane into the air. Here in Montgomery, however, there was plenty of room for the airplane to build up speed on takeoff, and an incline and weights would not be needed. Taylor also took some time to explain that the airplane was launched on a single-rail track and that airplanes took off into the wind. The track could be picked up and moved to face the wind.[142]

Taylor went on to underscore the popularity of flying. Demand was outstripping supply, he said, even though airplanes cost $7,500 apiece. Wealthy society men were especially keen on learning to fly as a sport. Taylor explained the situation in an exceptionally clear comparison:

> The aeroplane industry at present is in its infancy. Only a few years ago an automobile was considered a rich man's toy. Motor cars were not brought into commercial use, and only the wealthy could afford to buy them. 'Tis the same way with flying machines. Only the very wealthy, with a desire for the new sensation of aerial flights can and will invest in aeroplanes now. Perhaps this will be changed some day, but even under existing conditions the demand for aeroplanes is rapidly growing.[143]

The *Advertiser* made it its duty to act as eyes and ears for aviation-crazed Montgomerians. The reporter watched and described as "the great white mechanical bird" took shape. Very quickly the "planes" were in place. The two planes, each made of three sections, were held in place six feet apart and were kept parallel by wooden supports and wires. The outer edges of these planes, the newspaper explained, were sometimes called "wings." On March 22, the accompanying photograph of the Wrights' airplane at Fort Myer helped make it all clear. It was the first actual photo of a Wright airplane that the newspaper had obtained.[144]

Unfortunately, such detailed descriptions of the airplane weren't enough to satisfy Montgomery residents who were anxious to see the airplane in person. They sulked, and the *Advertiser*, in turn, sulked. The newspaper reported, "Although there were a number of visitors at the camp Monday, their curiosity was unsatisfied. Ropes prevented their entrance into the aeroplane shed, and their questions elicited no replies from the busy workers." That was frustrating enough, but it was impossible for the interested observer to find out anything on his own. According to the *Advertiser*, Montgomery residents had been "searching their dictionaries and encyclopedia in the hope of familiarizing themselves with aerial terms. Because of the recent advent of the industry, however, their quest has been in vain."[145] The reporter himself was in that boat and was embarrassed about his own ignorance of aviation, which had been splashed throughout the *Advertiser* for some weeks now. "What do you aeroplane folks call this building where you keep the machine?" he asked Taylor, who at last chose to answer a question. The newspaper had been calling the hangar an "aerie," but Taylor replied in a way that was sure to embarrass the aviation writer. "To be correct, I suppose it is called an 'aerodrome,'" Taylor said. "But we generally refer to it as a 'shed' or sometimes as the 'shack.' We use only plain English in our business, and the efforts of some ambitious writers to coin terms and phrases for us sometimes is amusing." At least the reporter had gotten other terms right. Taylor informed him that it was inappropriate to call an airplane an "airship." Airships were plodding dirigibles, which could be steered but were cumbersome. An airplane "is a flying machine in every sense of the word, and travels with the speed of an express train," he said.[146]

Smarting from the sting of being embarrassed as well as snubbed, the writer noted in the caption for the picture of the Fort Myer airplane that viewers could see "the long line of trolley cars in which thousands of spectators went to witness the flights."[147] That should remind the privacy-seeking airplane builders of the reality that privacy was just not possible for the greatest sport in town. Giving its readers another taste of the airplane as it had appeared at Fort Myer, the next day the *Advertiser* ran a different photo of that airplane. This time the caption noted that Confederate General Robert E. Lee's home could be seen in the background.[148] There was something to be said for keeping things in historic perspective in these dizzyingly modern times, after all.

Despite the Wright camp's refusal to answer questions, the Wright team was already bringing Montgomery much pride. San Jose, California, offered the Wright brothers $16,000 to exhibit the Wright Flyer in a four-day aviation meet there. Wilbur turned the city down. For one thing, he said in a March 23 interview with the Associated Press, he and Orville no longer

*Wilbur (left) and Orville Wright. Although the brothers were never in Montgomery together, they were photographed together in 1910 in this picture.*

flew for money, and for another, they were planning to go to the training grounds in Montgomery. "When our testing grounds are in readiness, we can make that amount in one week and therefore we wish to push that end of our work as rapidly as possible," Wilbur said, testifying to the monetary value of the Montgomery experience.[149] The brothers clearly valued the Alabama school for the future income it would bring when Montgomery-trained pilots would be available to exhibit flight and to teach sportsmen to fly their newly purchased airplanes. The money was in airplane sales and exhibitions, not in the $250-per-student tuition. The $250 covered any damage to the airplane as well. The schoolmasters weren't getting rich from tuition.[150]

Although it had been annoyed when the Wright crew gave its questions the cold shoulder, the *Advertiser* was smitten when Orville arrived in town on March 24. The paper exclaimed, full of celebrity worship, "Orville Wright, king of the air, hero of many a daring aerial exploit, and recipient of remarkable honors from royalty and citizenry alike, is in Montgomery!" Fred Ball of the Commercial Club met Orville and took him to lunch at the Exchange Hotel, where he and his crew were checked in.[151] The Exchange happened to be the nicest hotel in town. The seven-story building at the corner of Montgomery and Commerce streets featured the latest amenities, including a private ice plant (it made ten tons a day) and bay windows overlooking downtown in most of the 165 suites. The building was only two years old. The modern, steel-framed Exchange superseded the 1846 building that had housed Jefferson Davis and his congress during the first few months of the Confederacy. It was in the older version of the Exchange that the historic message was composed ordering freshly assembled Confederate troops to fire on Fort Sumter in 1861.[152]

But the Civil War was over, and all that remained of the old Exchange were legends. The new Exchange, playing host to the world leader in aviation, was heralding a new era in Montgomery. After Fred Ball took the newly arrived Orville to lunch at the Exchange, he escorted Orville to the brand new aviation camp. Characteristically and perhaps to some local surprise, Orville kept on his dressy business attire while he worked on the airplane.[153] Thirty-eight-year-old Orville was famous for his impeccable white collars as

*A very nice dormitory: The founder, professor, and students of the Wright pilot training school in Montgomery stayed at the new Exchange Hotel.*

well as his perfectly groomed mustache. He appeared to be more a gentleman than a man involved in repair of a large piece of machinery.

Orville had come to Montgomery because of its excellent weather, but Montgomery citizens were determined to show off the other things a person could do, besides fly airplanes, in the pleasant winter weather in the South. Ball invited Orville to dinner at his home, and there Orville was impressed to see 'Dorothy Perkins' climbing roses growing profusely that time of year. Another dinner guest that day, Judge William H. Thomas, invited Orville to the golf links, the very ones Wilbur had spared by ruling them out as a flying field. Orville had never golfed before, but Southern gentlemen can play golf while snow is on the ground up North, so he gave it a good try. At one point, the great aviator had to chase a stray ball and ran into a meadow lark's nest. The frightened bird feigned a broken wing to try to draw the intruders away from the nest, and Orville remarked that it was similar to the crippled wing of an airplane.[154] He had certainly seen a lot of those.

Orville was very much aware that he was the hero of the hour in Montgomery. He tried to feed some of the celebrity frenzy with facts. For instance, he announced, the airplane now being prepared for use in Montgomery was one of his company's oldest, perhaps the tenth it had produced, and had been in use for more than a year. Although the gossip around town was that he would be training military pilots, Orville assured everyone that he had no such orders. He would be training Spencer C. Crane, James Davis, and Walter Brookins to be company pilots. Those men, in turn, would be qualified to instruct society sportsmen who bought personal airplanes.[155]

That initial class of three started pretty close to home for teacher Orville. Brookins, who was just twenty-one and often sported a rakish bow tie, was called "Brookie" by the Wrights. Not surprisingly, he preferred the more mature-sounding "W. R. Brookins." To bachelors Wilbur and Orville, however, he was as close to a son as anyone could be. Brookie was a Dayton neighbor of the Wrights who had hung out first at the Wright bicycle shop and then at the Wright airplane works since he was age four. Orville had indulgently promised young Brookie his own airplane someday, and maybe the Montgomery school was a step in that direction. Completing the family tie, Brookie had been a student of the Wrights' sister, Katharine, at Dayton's Central High School.[156]

The next student at the brand new pilot school was also from Dayton. Despite the hometown connection, Spencer Crane was not nearly the pet that Brookie was. However, he had been with the Wrights for a fairly long time. When Orville first showed off the airplane for Army officials at Fort Myer, Virginia, in 1908, Crane was on hand as an automobile driver. He operated the car that pulled the military supply wagon that the airplane rode to the testing ground, while Orville stood on the auto's running board.[157]

The third student, James Davis, was from Colorado Springs, Colorado. Very little information has turned up on him.

It was within the *Montgomery Advertiser*'s rich imagination to speculate that perhaps Robert F. Collier, the New York publisher, and Russel A. Alger, a New York society figure, would also appear at the camp to learn to pilot airplanes themselves. The wishful thinking was based on the fact that

*Spencer Crane was probably the automobile driver pictured here as the Wright Flyer was pulled to the field at Fort Myer, Virginia, in 1908. The picture includes another aircraft—an Army balloon.*

both were stockholders in the Wright Company and were likely to buy an airplane anyway.[158]

Orville was aware of the public's distress about restrictions at his training camp. He no doubt also knew that Robert Collier was not on his way to Montgomery, nor was Russel Alger, and that, too, would cause celebrity-seeking flight fans in Montgomery some disappointment. Accordingly, Orville tried to smooth ruffled feathers. He foresaw a need to build a high fence around the camp to keep out spectators, or, in the absence of a fence, to establish a patrol around the airplane shed (as the *Advertiser* now usually called it). To stave off inevitable disappointment, he tried to explain the need from a European perspective. "When flights were made in Berlin, the field was patrolled by the police," Orville said. "The German people have very great respect for the police, and we were not bothered to any great extent . . . If the public wishes to come to the spring training camp, a patrol necessarily must be established."[159] Whether this explanation satisfied curiosity-seekers in Montgomery is doubtful, for eventually Orville couldn't stop the crowds of people making their way to the flying school to watch the pilots in action. For the moment, however, he had tried to create a buffer zone around his flight school, to keep its adoring fans at a distance.

*Advertiser* editor Screws was not among aviation's adoring fans, but he admitted that aviation was the greatest spectator sport that had ever landed in Montgomery—and accordingly, as he saw it, fans should hurry to the field. Screws noted in a March 26 opinion piece, "Pretty soon Montgomery will be having visitors from all over the country attracted by interest in the Wright Brothers flying machines. All the accessories for success in their enterprise are to be found here and close at hand."[160] Certainly the last sentence was meant to remind Orville that the accessories had been donated by Montgomerians who thus had a perfect right to see the airplane in action. To emphasize this important fact, another article announced that, despite the Wright camp's assertion that the aviators would *not* be staging exhibitions, the Mobile and Ohio Railroad had scheduled five shuttle trains running daily to the aviation camp for the convenience of spectators. To facilitate the important work of spectating, the daily Mobile and Ohio through train would also stop, on flag, at the camp each day.[161]

The *Advertiser* made little effort to hide its unhappiness with the Wrights' hands-off approach to spectators, and the aviation reporter was still sullen when Orville first flew the newly assembled airplane in a test flight on March 26. The reporter saw the flight, but few others did, a fact which the writer considered an affront to the locals who had anticipated seeing the great machine in the air. He seemed more than a little worried that perhaps no one at all would ever see the big bird fly. He groused, "There were few spectators. There had been no promise of flight made." So few onlookers were there that the reporter was able to list all eight white people on hand to watch. In a hasty phrase, he nodded to the fact that the black residents of the area were also among the first witnesses of the Wright brothers' flights in Alabama.[162] The black field hands worked Kohn's cotton acreage, probably as sharecroppers.[163]

While the *Advertiser* stood nervously in the door between the celebrity aviators and the gawking public, the *Birmingham Age-Herald* was having much more fun watching the pilot school unfold. The *Advertiser* grumbled about the behavior of Orville and his men, but the *Age-Herald's* reporter seemed to get along fine with the airmen. The Birmingham newspaper noted admiringly: "Mr. Wright is a hard worker himself. He does not come in for

*The great white bird flew low over Kohn's cotton fields.*

lunch, taking a 'snack' out in a paper box, so that he can be on the ground all the time and see just what is being done."[164] *Age-Herald* reporter Hervey W. Laird seemed to know a lot more about the Wright brothers than their Montgomery hosts did. He commented:

> Just to look at Orville Wright one would not take him to be a man who, with a wonderful invention, has startled the world. He is a modest sort of fellow with a cordial smile and fraternal temperament and seems to be quite fond of people. He talks interestingly of the many countries where his machines have been exhibited and has found much to entertain him outside his airship investigations.
>
> The Wright family is well known to many in Alabama. An elder brother has property in Birmingham, or did have, and he has been often down south. Orville Wright, however, is on his first trip to this section and among other things, he is very anxious to see cotton growing.[165]

Furthermore, unlike the *Advertiser*'s writer, Laird knew something about aviation. He described the Wright staff as installing a "rear portion" on the airplane, which he then described as "somewhat the nature of a tail, in which the rudder will be held."[166] The term "tail" never did occur in the *Advertiser*, which tended to refer to the tail section as "planes," just like the wings. Laird was clearly more familiar with aircraft lingo. Revealing further his familiarity with airplanes, Laird added, "There is ever so much more of this part [the tail] of the machine than before, and it is anticipated that it will add

*The Wright biplane is positioned on its monorail track for a Montgomery takeoff. The rear horizontal stabilizer was added to the Wright airplane in Montgomery. It was the most significant technological change in the airplane since Kitty Hawk.*

greatly to the handling of the apparatus in mid-air."[167] Laird had noticed the addition of a horizontal stabilizer on the rear of the Montgomery airplane. The Alabama Flyer, indeed, was the first Wright airplane to feature a rear stabilizer.[168] Clearly Laird knew what the Wright Flyer had once looked like and was familiar enough to notice a difference as the aircraft had evolved over time. He also understood the principles that governed flight, realizing that the stabilizer would allow better control.

Aviation business aside, Laird boldly asked Orville about Ohio politics. "Mr. Wright is a good talker on politics and is especially interesting in his opinions of the state of Ohio," Laird reported. Orville felt that Ohioans were "badly out with President Taft," and he ventured to predict who might win the next presidential election.[169]

Laird grew even bolder. Had Orville been shaken by his crash at Fort Myer, which had killed his passenger, Lieutenant Thomas E. Selfridge? Orville said he had not been and explained the peculiarities that had caused the crash to be fatal.[170]

Two days after the first flight, when the big bird flew again, the *Adver-*

*tiser* reported with satisfaction on something like a battle won. More than one hundred people had trekked to the Kohn plantation to witness the miracle of flight—a turnout that was displayed prominently in the article's secondary headline: "Hundred People Watch Flight Monday." This time the reporter did showcase the fact that the black field workers were among the witnesses to the important event:

> Up one hundred feet above the dingy negro cabins and fields of brown stubble, the aeroplane of Orville Wright soared Monday afternoon, west of Montgomery on the Washington Ferry Road, and more than a hundred people gasped as the gigantic kite sailed to the accompaniment of staccato explosions of its gasoline engine. The airplane engine exhibited a perverse spirit and after each flight the aeronaut was forced to alight because a gear had slipped or an exhaust valve was plugged. Seldom before, according to the assistants of Mr. Wright, has the engine gone wrong, but Monday afternoon all the pent-up stubbornness of months was evident from the behavior of the machine.[171]

It was clear that the *Advertiser*'s reporter had been assigned the airplane beat for his powers of description, so that he could pass along the full glory of Montgomery's newest sport to readers who might not be so fortunate as to attend the pilot training sessions in person. Now that so many spectators were indeed finding their way to the new Wright field, the reporter no longer felt obliged to grumble about the lack of witnesses. Instead, he was in his poetic element, quite happy to have something to describe after much "pent-up stubbornness of months" (or weeks, anyway) on his own part of waiting for a flight to happen. The writer gloried in discussion of flight. "The spectacular feature of the flight Monday came at the sharp turn which the aeroplane took in changing its course," he wrote. "In turning, the airship inclined upon one end, sometimes almost to the point where it seemed that it would capsize. At all times during the flight the machine went up and down, pitched and swerved, as a ship on the water." Each time Orville flew over, the audience applauded, but tensed when the airplane dipped to within ten feet of the ground, all of them half expecting to see a crack-up in the cotton field.[172]

Such reports only drew more Montgomerians to the flying field. Clearly there was going to have to be an arrangement with Orville about spectators at camp; the crowds simply wanted to be there. Window-viewing from nearby houses wasn't good enough, nor were limited visits on designated spectator days. Thus, the Commercial Club met with Orville and got him to agree that the public would be welcome as long as no one interfered with the work. Visitors had to stay off the field, for instance, and no one would be allowed in the shed. Spectators would have to stay in a roped-off area. "As no charge will be made, no seats or other conveniences can be furnished," the *Advertiser* explained to readers.[173]

In contrast to the *Advertiser*'s continual hand-wringing over the rights of the fans, the *Age-Herald* was little bothered about any restrictions at the camp. In fact, it made Orville sound very welcoming. Quoting an interview with Orville, the *Age-Herald*'s special correspondent Laird reported that the great aviator himself would be flying on every fine day. Orville told Laird that crowds could nearly depend on seeing him in the air when the weather was good. "Those who care to go to the grounds will be welcome," Laird assured his Birmingham readers.[174] Montgomerians felt they had unfairly been restricted from camp, but Birmingham readers certainly had no clue of any restrictions.

Visitors to the camp, welcome or not, were hoping to see Orville fly, of course. However, they could more likely count on seeing students, and then only in the right conditions. Orville could fly in any ordinary wind, but his students needed light winds only, about six to eight miles per hour. High winds confused new pilots, who were often unclear whether it was their actions or the wind that caused bounces in the airplane. "Aeroplane sailing, it is explained, is not all mere manipulation of the engine," the *Advertiser* tried to explain to its readers. "There [are] judgments of currents to be taken, balancing to be gauged, and a dozen other little niceties of piloting that will come only with practice."[175]

On March 29, engine trouble grounded the airplane. A valve head in the second cylinder came loose and broke the piston. The problem occurred many feet aloft, but Orville landed the airplane without shaking himself or Brookins from their seats. The flying ended for the day while the aviators figured out the trouble. The resulting frustrations unconsciously showed the intersection of history, as measured in modes of transportation. The *Advertiser* reported, "Visitors, coming out on the shuttle train and in automobiles and buggies were disappointed when informed that there would be no flight during the day." The engine couldn't be repaired without awaiting parts, so Orville and his party took off to see some of Montgomery in a private automobile.[176]

The airplane crew didn't even bother to come to work for the next two days, looking around town informally while they waited for their needed parts to arrive. The *Advertiser*'s reporter couldn't wait for flight training to resume. He hung out at the Exchange Hotel until he ran into Orville, who told him then that it would take four hours to fix the broken engine parts— if the lagging parts would ever get to Montgomery. In a jovial mood that day, Orville commented that Wilbur had written him a letter that kidded Orville about turning a cartwheel in the airplane in mid-air. Apparently, the cartwheel story had been given out by the press in Ohio, explaining falsely why the Montgomery airplane had been grounded. As Orville explained it, a lot of people failed to understand airplanes and thus spread all sorts of wild rumors. Reports of accidents in newspapers, like the false reports of the cartwheel, were almost always exaggerated.[177]

"He said that an aeroplane cannot turn over or fall when the motor breaks or stops, but that the aeroplane simply glides," the *Advertiser*'s reporter wrote, trying to make sense of it all.[178] The *Advertiser* did have cause for some professional pride in the matter. Unlike the Ohio press, its own reports were accurate; *its* reporter had never described a cartwheel.

The theory that airplanes were safe in an accident, however, was not as convincing as the Prince of the Air made it seem. Perhaps in another case of misinformed reporting, the press covering aviation in San Sebastian, Spain, described the death of French aviator Hubert Leblon in terms not unlike Wilbur's joking letter. "He was circling the Royal Palace of Miramar at a height of 140 feet, when his motor broke down," the report ran. "He attempted to glide to the shed but the machine turned over and swooped with terrific

*Top, Lieutenant Thomas Selfridge awaits a flight with Orville in Fort Myer, Virginia, in 1908. A few minutes later, Selfridge became the world's first fatality in a motorized fixed-wing aircraft. Bottom, Selfridge died in this crash, with Orville in the pilot's seat.*

force against the rocks. The aviator was crushed like an eggshell." The article went on to make a grim tally: Since the invention of the airplane, a total of four people had been killed in airplane accidents, including Orville Wright's own passenger, Lieutenant Selfridge. Orville, for his part, was adamant that a Wright machine never could flip over as Leblon's had.[179]

Unfortunately, the next day brought more bad news. The German dirigible *Pommern* blew into the Baltic Sea, killing three men, including Reichstag member Werner Hugo Del Brueck, who, along with another in the party, drowned. A fourth man was in serious condition. Del Brueck himself had been piloting. Sadly, the craft had landed due to hurricane conditions, when it broke away before it was fully secured. The *Pommern* was swept up into the sky, collided with a factory roof, and then plunged into the sea.[180] Then the next day the press listed, as it called him, "the latest victim"—German professor Richard Abegg, who was killed while attempting to land a hot-air balloon. The professor was getting out of the basket, when the wind swept it across the ground, crushing his skull and legs. He died shortly thereafter.[181]

The ongoing tragedies marked a run of terrible luck, one that might have dampened flying fever in Montgomery. The bad news certainly had that effect on the editor of the *Advertiser*, W. W. Screws, who commented pointedly, "Aviation is adding another to human dangers . . . The truth is that aviation is yet in its infantile stage." Screws warned that machinery could not be made perfect, and even if it could, human pilots could not be perfect, nor could the weather be held to a constant standard of perfection. "At present flying is a rather dangerous pastime, especially for the careless and unwary," he snarled.[182]

His comment seemed to be based on the rash of aircraft fatalities, but five days later he got more specific and betrayed a dislike of the Wright brothers at the root of his sourness on aviation. He decried the Wrights' never-ending patent infringement cases, which were dampening the ability of many United States aviators to fly. "It is intimated that the time will come when one corporation or company of inventors and manufacturers of flying machines will be able to monopolize the entire business, and all others who fly will have to procure licenses from the boss organization," Screws wrote, obviously referring to the famous guests of his city. "We would consider it the height of absurdity if one great steamship company . . . should set up a claim to control of the oceans and seas, and require all other people to procure a license or permit from the self-constituted controllers of the waters." Such a tyranny in the air was just as ridiculous, he said. "The fact is that this talk about controlling the air seems absurd, at least at this stage of the game," Screws scoffed. "When aviation becomes common, if it ever does, it may be that there will be laws enacted regarding it, but we hardly expect the time will ever come when a man or company will try to obtain an exclusive license to carry on the business."[183]

In still another editorial, the *Advertiser* indicated that not everyone in Montgomery was as wild about aviation as it seemed. Not everyone necessarily wanted to come out to the aviation camp, and not everyone was hanging on every word uttered (or not uttered) by the Wright crew. Screws commented that the United States was a nation of doubters, and he certainly numbered himself among those, Wrights or no Wrights. "Even now there are many who laugh at the bare thought that aviation will ever be a practical method of travel. We all know that much has been done in this comparatively new business; that many wonderful flights have been made, but there are some of us who are slow to believe that it will ever be what its advocates claim for it," he said. Screws did allow, however, that he might be destined to be convinced.[184]

In a sharp contrast in outlook, E. W. Barrett, the editorial writer for the *Birmingham Age-Herald,* pointed out that curmudgeonly Mr. Screws was missing the fact that it was Montgomery, not just the Wrights, which was now the spectated—not merely the spectator—in the great sport of aviation. "Some cities achieve greatness and some have greatness thrust upon 'em," the Birmingham writer quipped, digging at Montgomery just a little. The *Age-Herald* editor saw Montgomery as "the envy of all other cities, and the pride of America." Each flight, he said, made Montgomery more glorious. He called the conquest of the air the "chief event of the century" and predicted that Montgomery would go down in history "as the scene of the world's progress in a great achievement." Finally he issued a challenge for Montgomery, a pretty stiff one that might have been exciting, had Montgomery taken it up. "Montgomery," the *Age-Herald* said, "should rise to the occasion by organizing a great American [airplane] meet that would call together all American aero clubs, and encourage experimental work."[185]

It is intriguing to think that Birmingham might have taken up the bold challenge issued in its own newspaper. The city would no doubt have been delighted to host the Wright pilot school—but alas, Birmingham was far too mountainous for student pilots.

*Orville and his students check over the biplane after windy weather had grounded it. On the roof at left, note the two students, who perhaps had climbed up to check on the wind velocity.*

# 4

# THE PROFESSOR AT WORK

I f skeptics needed convincing that aviation was viable, then Orville
Wright was the man to convince them, once the replacement parts
arrived for his stubborn engine. Orville chose to ignore a spell of bad
weather, because he was anxious to get on with the business at hand. Amid
gusty on-again, off-again showers on April 1, Orville took to the skies as
soon as the motor was repaired. The five flights "demanded every particle
of the aviator's skill," the *Advertiser's* admiring aviation reporter described.
Orville was not exactly reckless in the matter—he sent Brookins and Davis
more than once to the rooftop of the shed to gauge the wind speed. When
the weather cleared up, nervousness evaporated and the picture was awe-
inspiring. As crowds watched, white sunlight glinted off the wings. Orville
dipped the airplane to within a few feet of the onlookers, letting it skim
along at eye level. In one of the earliest recorded instances of a near miss in
an airplane, two very surprised sparrows barely escaped being run down by
Orville's craft and flapped madly out of the way.[186]

Unexpectedly on another day, Orville ran into what he called "whirlwinds." These, thankfully, were not the dreaded tornado type but rather were
invisible, whirling circles of air that did strange things to the airplane. Orville
was quite a distance off the ground on a sunny day in Montgomery when
he ran into the first whirlwind. He suddenly could not make the airplane
descend. "I remained at a height of about fifteen hundred feet for a period
of five minutes. Suddenly the machine [airplane] began to descend and was
on the ground in less than a minute," he said. Other than the whirlwind
that had ensnared the airplane, the wind had been perfectly calm that day.

Orville was used to little whirlwinds of one hundred feet across, but this one, Orville said, was especially large, and "the air was rising as fast as the machine could descend."[187] As one of Orville's students complained, the "nasty little whirlwinds" were more common in Montgomery than anywhere else he had ever seen. He eagerly awaited their cessation.[188]

To add to those troubles, the airplane's motor kept running poorly. Orville noted that he had never had such trouble with the twelve other motors he had used. A frustrated Orville tried to make the most of the never-ending problems. "What we are working for now is reliability in the aeroplane," he said as cheerfully as possible. "We are still experimenting on the motors for the aeroplane and when the reliability of this motor is established I expect they will be found more reliable than the automobile motor." Continuing in that train of thought, Orville predicted that airplanes would one day be used to carry mail and that they "would be used for quick journeys in the place of a special train and for personal recreation." He deftly sidestepped a reporter's question about airplanes being used for war, but he did offer a correct prediction that airplanes would not make automobiles obsolete. The domain of the automobile and the domain of the airplane were quite different, Orville explained.[189]

With all eyes still on the Montgomery airfield and nothing much to report except an airplane still grounded by engine trouble, the *Advertiser* hung onto Orville's every word to keep the public's thirst for aviation news satisfied. A traveling salesman from Boston chatted with Orville on one slow day at the Exchange. He asked Orville why he had chosen Montgomery. The airman replied that the late winter and early spring in the South offered better weather than Ohio did for his work.[190] Not that it hadn't been said before, but anything from the world's most famous pilot and teacher of aviation seemed worth repeating in the *Advertiser*, since nothing much else was happening at the school. The salesman asked how long it took to train a pilot, and Orville offered the information that it could be done in just two days, given the flexibility and attentiveness of his pupils. Just that day, in fact, he had added a pupil, Archibald Hoxsey, a tall, bespectacled twenty-five-year-old California auto racer sent to Montgomery by Roy Knabenshue, who was the Wright Company's newly hired contract manager.[191] Knabenshue

*Orville and his students no doubt enjoyed Court Square Fountain,*
*which had been a Montgomery landmark for decades.*

had suspected Hoxsey would make an excellent pilot after the young man
tuned up the engine of a dirigible airship that Knabenshue flew at one of
his state fair exhibitions.[192] Apparently the ability to make repairs to aircraft
was key to flying them. As any of the aviators in Montgomery could attest,
flying machines did break down a lot.

Orville finally got fed up with the recalcitrant engine and took the thing
to pieces. Upon inspection, he decided to send to Dayton for replacement
parts. Unable to fly, Orville and his pupils decided at last, on April 6, to
see their host city in true tourist fashion with a formal, organized tour.
Montgomery proudly showed off its finest attractions. The *Advertiser*'s aviation reporter trailed the group as it visited the Capitol. "Here Mr. Wright

*Montgomery's cutting-edge electric system was the envy of the world in 1910. Here a maze of wires festoons the air above Court Square. Such a sight caused Spencer Crane to declare Montgomery a lively and progressive city.*

found a number of persons connected with the State administration on the historic steps, busily engaged in looking for the strange star that had been 'discovered' near to the moon," the newspaper reported. In fact, one of the men happened to be Governor Braxton Bragg Comer, to whom Orville was introduced. "Mr. Wright succeeded in locating the star for the Governor, and then announced it was his opinion that it was Venus," the newspaper said. The article added seriously, "and as he had been closer to that star than anyone present, his word was readily accepted."[193] Such was the status of the Hero of the Heavens.

Orville met other officials at the Capitol building, and he was reverently shown the very spot where Jefferson Davis had stood when he was inaugurated president of the Confederate States of America. The visit marked an interesting juxtaposition of the past that had so recently weighed Alabama down, coupled with the future that could catapult it into the skies. At that moment in 1910, the Civil War met the future. In the eyes of many of Orville's earnest fans, the old notions embedded in the Civil War were melting away. Orville, too, seemed to feel that way. After the tour, he commented that he was "greatly pleased" with Montgomery and was actually surprised at how picturesque it was and at how energetic its citizens were[194]—no doubt the old stereotype of the lazy Southerner having been in his thought.

One of Orville's pupils, Spencer Crane, endeared himself to everyone by speaking of how pleased he was with Montgomery. He had tried, back in Dayton, to look up the city, but all he could discover was that it was the capital of Alabama—nor could his acquaintances tell him anything more than that. "Mr. Crane said he was greatly surprised at the electrical display in this city, and that he was convinced by it that he had come to a lively spot," the *Advertiser* beamed. Crane also visited the new city wharf and toured the wholesale district, along with the Capitol and residential areas. "He stands ready to endorse Montgomery as a city of progress, of beauty, and a great business center," the paper announced proudly.[195] This was what the *Advertiser* had envisioned all along; this was the Montgomery the Commercial Club had wanted the world to see through the aviators' admiring eyes.

In addition to that much-craved glory for the city, Orville now indicated that the time spent in Montgomery had assured him of a vitally important fact: apparently anyone with normal intelligence could become a pilot. None of Orville's current pupils had graduated yet, but that didn't seem to matter in his summary of the Montgomery flying school so far. Orville did suggest, however, that mechanics or chauffeurs might have a natural advantage in learning to fly. Also, one of the critical requirements of operating airplanes at present was being male. Orville said he and Wilbur had had countless applications from women who wanted flying lessons, "but we have thought it best to ignore them. Many of the applications were made by women looking for notoriety. We are not conducting a circus or a show and for this reason we have decided not to teach women, who want only to get into the limelight," he said.[196]

If any women were disappointed about this, the *Advertiser* ignored them. Instead the newspaper bestowed upon Orville the title "professor of flying," noting that no such title actually existed, but the *Advertiser* felt that the great inventor had earned the title through his school in Montgomery. After granting the honorary doctorate, the newspaper noted that Orville was the first professor of flying that "America has ever boasted."[197] In the very next article, a student of Wright rival Glenn Curtiss received an ovation for his first public flight,[198] but there were no plaudits from the *Advertiser* nor any recognition given to "professor" Curtiss.

Meanwhile there was a widespread rumor that Orville would send for a second airplane for the Montgomery school. This he would neither confirm nor deny. "I couldn't say just now whether we will ship another bi-plane to Montgomery. It is possible that later we will, although much flying can be done with one machine," Orville said, having learned to handle the press's queries with a clever sort of evasion associated with politicians. Nor would he directly respond to the reporter's broad hint that maybe the Wright Company would open a second airplane manufacturing facility in Montgomery. Orville said diplomatically, "Whether we will establish other factories in various parts of the United States I am unable to say at present. Our factory at Dayton is large enough to meet all demands for the present, at any rate. Of course in time it will probably be necessary to equip other factories, but this will not be done for some time. At present the demand for aeroplanes is limited."[199]

Orville did, however, see a great scope for aviation yet to come. "There is no limit to the possibilities of the aeroplane," Orville predicted for Montgomery readers. "When the demand justifies it, we will be in a position to supply machines with carrying possibilities greatly in excess of those today." He added that at present his airplanes could carry four people, if the buyer wanted them equipped with that many seats. He foresaw airplanes carrying even more passengers, someday.[200]

As any newspaper reader could tell, Orville's welcoming adulation from Montgomery was a great boon to aviation, compared to France's harsh treatment of its pilots. Under the headline "France Also Has a Flying School," the *Advertiser* restrained itself from chest-thumping about Montgomery's enthusiastic reception of the Wright school. In Chalons, France, Henri Farman's flying school had run afoul of the military. One of the Frenchmen, piloting an Antoinette airplane, flew beyond the aerodrome and over a military installation. The military commander there, distressed by his base's vulnerability, issued orders that no airplanes were to fly out of the aerodrome grounds, and he limited the times airplanes could be in the air. "A cross-country practice is seriously impeded by these restrictions," the writer pointed out. Furthermore, the foreigners attracted to Chalons to view the flights caused the military men to fear espionage, a worry that had yet to rear its head in Montgomery. The French military suspected that Farman's students were actually spies trying to peek at the army base below. As a result of all the restrictions, Farman was moving his school elsewhere.[201] It surely didn't take half a thought for Montgomery readers to glow with pride at the comparison. Although there had been some disappointments at first about not seeing the Wrights fly, there was nothing like the intrigue and distastefulness being suffered by Farman. Indeed, no one had to worry about any military installation being spied upon in Montgomery, as that Army base the city was fighting for had not yet materialized.

Meanwhile, Orville headed back to Dayton on April 8 to overhaul the stubborn airplane motor. Gossip around Montgomery once again suggested that Orville would bring a second airplane back with him. When one airplane was down, the other would be up, and lots of lost time would thereby be found, rumors said.[202] And, thank goodness, Montgomery's perplexing whirlwinds were expected to subside by the time Orville got back. The *Advertiser* poetically calculated that "the milder touch of spring" would thus facilitate "the angelic art of flying" by eliminating the whirlwinds.[203]

Indeed, the angelic art of flying needed all the help it could get. Not so very far away in Memphis, Tennessee, an air show featuring airplanes licensed by the patent-holding Wrights ended dramatically when J. C. Mars's airplane crashed into an automobile. The three women and two children inside the auto were saved by the unlikely barrier of the vehicle's canvas canopy roof. Mars had slight injuries, but his biplane went to pieces. In fact, it may have been something like the Montgomery whirlwinds that put such a ghastly end to Memphis's first air show. Apparently Mars was caught in a sudden wind gust, spinning his airplane around and throwing him at right angles to his original destination. Spectators screamed when they realized that the airplane would smash into the automobile, and although the ladies and children inside the vehicle saw the airplane coming, they didn't have time to leap clear. Instead they threw themselves onto the floor. The airplane actually hit the hood of the car and fell over onto the canopy, which spared the auto's helpless occupants.[204]

At least Memphis had airplanes to see. Montgomery was playing a waiting game. Orville took much longer than he had planned to overhaul the airplane's distressing motor. After more than a week, Montgomery at last got word that the motor and Orville were heading back to town. By now everyone had figured out that the Wrights would not send a second airplane to Montgomery. However, the famous brothers did send a new set of wings to replace those on the Montgomery airplane, and by now a fifth student had been added to the roster. Besides Spencer Crane and W. R. Brookins, Arch Hoxsey was still there, as was James Davis. The new student was Arthur L. Welsh, who had seen Orville fly at Fort Myer, Virginia, in 1908 and had become interested in flying himself. Although he now hailed from Washington, D.C., the twenty-eight-year-old Welsh offered a touch of the exotic to the pilot class of 1910—he was a Jew originally from Russia, born just outside of Kiev.[205] Not surprisingly, many other men had been applying to the Wright school as well. Swallowing disappointment about the lack of a second airplane, the *Advertiser* supported the Wrights' decision to turn down the many applicants. "With one aeroplane and one instructor, a larger class might prove unwieldy," the newspaper reasoned.[206]

It turned out to be worth Montgomery's wait for Orville to return from Ohio. On April 21, the nation's foremost professor of flying was back in the pilot's seat. To test the new motor, he tried the hard stuff. "Not only did Mr. Wright pilot his machine through a stiff breeze, gusty at best, but he made his starts at right angles to the wind and alighted with the greatest ease and precision," the *Advertiser*'s aviation reporter marveled, by now understanding the punishment the lightweight airplane endured in winds.

*When eras collide: Spectators who got to the flying field by horse and buggy were admonished to keep the creatures at home. It was better to take an automobile or the train to see the airplane. Horses were easily spooked by the flying machine.*

Orville circled thirty feet in the air but dipped down close enough to raise a cloud of dust. He came down quickly, after just four minutes, afraid that the motor would balk. The motor didn't, as it turned out, but horses did. In another point of contact between the pioneer age and the air age, a number of people had come by buggy to see Orville fly that Thursday. Unfortunately, the sound of the motor and the low flights terrified the animals, who were dangerously spooked and might have caused havoc had they gotten away. "In the future," the *Advertiser* scolded, "it will be necessary for those driving horses to leave them close to the aeroplane shed or on the main road. Under no circumstances will they be allowed at any point on the course."[207] It was, perhaps, a fitting dismissal of the nineteenth century. Horses were passé. The airplane would become the transportation of choice in the modern world.

Orville's flights only got better. Next day a huge crowd came (presumably sans horses) to watch him fly. The crowed applauded when he showed off the entire repertoire—graceful sweeps, quick turns—dipping groundward, climbing high, tracing a figure eight several times. The crowd had spent the entire afternoon behind the rope, waiting long, long hours to witness a flight. The airplane's clutches needed to be removed and reworked during the day, and that took some time. Of course, there had been the student flights in the morning, which were by nature low and unspectacular. Orville's work that evening at last was the prize, one that did not disappoint.[208]

Meanwhile, W. R. Brookins was making much progress as a student. Young Mr. Brookins was getting so good at piloting that Orville let him operate the elevator and even land the airplane once. Brookins was certainly the teacher's pet. Near dusk on April 22, Brookins and Orville made the longest flight of the day and stayed aloft ten minutes. The other students, however, spent a grueling afternoon learning to balance the machine on its monorail starting track.[209]

Montgomerians who stuck around all day to see the great Orville in action went away satisfied. City boosters were even more satisfied to discover

*A photo taken at Fort Myer, Virginia, shows the monorail starting track. Wright students spent many tedious hours learning to balance the airplane on the track.*

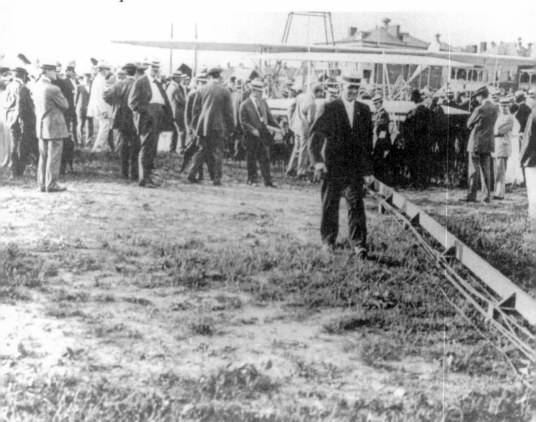

that Montgomery was, indeed, the envy of the world, as they had fervently hoped. Budapest, Hungary, let it be known that Orville would attend an aviation meet there in June to the tune of $50,000, a statement that Orville scoffed at. He had been courted by Budapest some time ago while he was in Germany, but he had turned the city down.[210] Thus, Montgomery outshone Budapest, no small achievement for a smallish city in the American Deep South.

But all was not entirely well. There was such a huge interest among Montgomerians and others in seeing a flight and so much down time for the airplane that there was a nagging, ongoing fear that guests would be turned away—horses had been banned, after all, and who knew but that people would be next? Sam J. Cassels, the new president of the Business Men's League in Montgomery (the Commercial Club reorganized and renamed),[211] accordingly went to the Wright camp to talk over the needs of spectators. If he went into the meeting to pressure Orville, however, Cassels was won over, even though the same old rules remained in place. Maybe they needed reiterating. Cassels reported them but then added his own tantalizing description that was sure to draw even more people to the airfield:

After a very delightful interview with the great aviator, I am authorized to say to the people of Montgomery and to the great number of visitors who are expected here during the next few weeks, and to say it upon the authority of Mr. Wright himself, that the public is entirely welcome at the demonstrations as often, and in as large numbers as may desire to go out. The only stipulation Mr. Wright makes is that no one shall cross the ropes and thereby interfere with the handling of the aeroplane in preparation for flights or in lighting.

I had the privilege of seeing two flights of the wonderful machine, one made by Mr. Wright alone, and the other accompanied by one of his pupils. No one can appreciate the marvel of this invention until he experiences the sensation [of seeing] the graceful mounting into the air of the bi-plane and see under what perfect control Mr. Wright has it—sees it describe any kind of figure through the air, now way over the tops of the houses and trees, now skimming along the surface as if trying to pluck the flowers from the field. Everybody in the state should see the wonderful bird.[212]

And of course, there was the requisite lauding of Montgomery: "It is a great thing for Montgomery that our city has been selected as the Wrights' field of operation for a season, and it serves as another plain evidence that we have a great city," Cassels said.[213]

The next day was Sunday, and there was never any flying at the Wright camp on Sundays,[214] but Cassels' desire to push visitors out to camp took a big blow on Monday, April 25. In a true shocker, it snowed! Snow was rare enough in Montgomery in high winter, and the Wrights had come from Dayton specifically to avoid snow—but here it was, nearly May, and *snow*, of all things, had done all sorts of mischief beyond just ruining the plans of the South's favorite civilian aircraft crew. Most seriously, the snow had wrecked the South's young cotton crop. An anguished agricultural observer, assessing damage to the entire Cotton Belt, declared that the South had had "its most disastrous financial setback perhaps since the civil war." It was the first snow ever recorded in Alabama in April—and some areas got sleet as well.[215]

In Montgomery itself, the snow wasn't as awful as it was out on the farms. Snow fell for three hours, melting as it fell on roofs or streets. Areas slightly north of Montgomery suffered one to four inches of accumulation[216]—as always, causing paralysis in the South. The intrepid, if astonished, aviators from Dayton figured that an Alabama snowfall couldn't last long and made the trip to the Kohn plantation through the flurries. The hardy airmen lit a roaring bonfire to keep warm. Apparently Orville and his students were surprised that the snow kept coming—surely as surprised as Montgomerians were. One of air crew had a camera, "and in a swirl of snow, he and several companions went forth to secure views of scenery in the 'Sunny South' in April 1910," the *Advertiser* reported.[217]

Finally the flight school had to shut down for a snow day, just like every other school in Alabama does when it snows. "Snowstorms and aerial operations do not go well together," the *Advertiser* explained to its readers. "At least, this was the conclusion reached by Orville Wright and his student

*Orville in flight over Montgomery. "Everybody in the state should see the wonderful bird," said Business Men's League President Sam J. Cassels.*

aviators Monday." The aviators went home to the Exchange Hotel at noon. Luckily, the weather was already moderating.[218]

In fact, as was generally expected in the South, the snow was gone the next day, and Orville made a flight of nineteen minutes, setting a local record for time aloft. Meanwhile, Brookins was getting good enough to fly the airplane entirely except during take-off. The excitement of the snowstorm had passed, and crowds of spectators from all over the place were at the camp again. They were treated to some of the realities of airplane travel of the era—a wire broke and had to be replaced after the airplane jumped its starting track. When the wind got too high, onlookers could only watch the student pilots learn to balance the craft on the track, as there could be no flights.[219] All those efforts did seem rather puny shortly, as word came that Louis Paulhan, the French aviator, had flown 186 miles from London to Manchester, England. Of course, he did have to stop over night in Lichfield, but the feat garnered him the $50,000 prize offered by Lord Northcliffe, an aviation supporter and newspaperman using his vast monetary resources to encourage flyers to push the limits.[220]

With such big money flying around in England, it was a bad day for Wright airplanes in the United States. Orville and Brookins were making a flight, when the motor began to skip. The resulting noise sounded pretty awful pretty quickly, and Orville made an attempt to land. When the motor recovered, he tried to fly on to the shed. Alas, however, the engine decided it couldn't go that far and stopped. As Orville had promised it would, the big bird glided to the ground gently, without really crashing, although the right wing hit the ground and was damaged. The airplane was only a few feet off the ground during the crisis, thus, onlookers thought, saving the pilots any serious injury. The engine again—it was so frustrating. The Wright camp hoped that all that was needed was a new magneto[221]—the dynamo that sparked the ignition. Meanwhile, in San Antonio, a lieutenant learning to fly the government's Wright airplane smashed a skid of the craft after a minor crash. Both pilot and passenger were shaken up but unhurt after a fall from a thankfully low distance of twenty feet. The pilot, Benjamin

*The only other airplane besides Montgomery's that was legally in operation in the United States in the spring of 1910. Army officers were learning to fly it in San Antonio, Texas.*

D. Foulois, expressed joy that the Army had recently required that Army airplanes would henceforth be fitted with wheels instead of skids. No doubt landings would be easier, and take-offs could be made without the monorail track system used by Wright Flyers up until that time.[222]

The Wright airplanes' crashes may have looked pathetic next to Paulhan's achievement, but Montgomery promoters didn't think so. As the best flights of the season were surely upcoming, and with the students really learning the knack of flying, plans were afoot to charter package railroad tours to the aviation camp from Birmingham, ninety miles away, and Mobile, way down near the Gulf of Mexico at one hundred seventy miles away.[223] The Business Men's League's board of directors made arrangements to advertise Montgomery specifically as the only place people could see Orville Wright in the air. The directors frankly admitted they hoped to bring thousands of visitors to Montgomery. And now the whole issue took on a new urgency. The Wright team announced it would not be staying permanently. No one knew how long they'd be there, but in the next few weeks, it seemed, the flyers would pack up for Dayton.[224]

Prodded by news that the Wright pilots would soon fly away, more and more crowds took carriages, automobiles, and trains to the camp on Washington Ferry Road. More than one thousand spectators watched as Orville himself put the airplane through its maneuvers on April 28, again trying to test the airplane after the old magneto was put back into it. At first he flew six hundred feet over spectators' craned necks. On another excursion, he flew more than 1,000 feet in the air. The huge crowd burst into cheers. A worried audience member quaked, "Do you suppose he will come down again?"[225]

After all the tussles with the engine, at last Orville's pupils figured out the trouble. "The Standard [Oil Company] has been giving us a bad lot of fuel," Orville complained frankly. His students had solved the problem, and he was grateful. "I thought we never were going to get past motor difficulties and bad weather," Orville said. He cleaned out the tank and ordered new gasoline. Now that the situation was corrected, the flying machine "behaved like a well-broken horse," he said.[226] The students' flights could only get better, and the same was true for the professor's flights. Now that

*Orville and his star student Walter Brookins prepare for a flight in Montgomery.*

Orville could fly pretty much uninterrupted by mechanical failure, spectators clamored to see the great teacher at work.

On the weekend of April 30, so many spectators showed up to watch Orville fly that the aviators had to double the roped enclosure to allow that many more visitors. By some estimates, three thousand people were crammed into the enclosure at the field on any given day.[227] Thousands watched as Orville worked some time to lower the wingtips about four or five inches, matching the settings he had used in earlier exhibition flights. Certainly he meant to show off, and he did, traveling by circles higher and higher until he outstripped his previous record for height aloft. The day became even more exciting when Brookins made his first complete flight as pilot, with Orville as passenger.[228] Meanwhile, more glory fell upon the Wright Company when the British navy reported a "novel experience"—a Wright-built airplane suddenly appeared from a bank of haze and danced around the ships below. Clearly showing the airplane's value for reconnaissance, pilot Cecil Grace then flew back to land, having flown fifty miles in fifty-one minutes.[229]

There was nothing Orville could do to dampen the adulation from his admiring public in Montgomery. He obligingly had his class of student pilots pose for a photo that ran in the *Advertiser*. The Mobile and Ohio resumed its shuttle service, and the flyers guaranteed a good view of their work now. Visitors were expected from all over Alabama and the adjoining states in the next weeks. The Wright crew was apparently far less worried about spectators now. Perhaps the crew had just gotten used to them. Then again, the new, more welcoming approach to spectators at the school also might have been fueled by the fact that W. R. Brookins was at last all but certified as a pilot and as an instructor. The nerve-wracking work of teaching a student to handle an airplane with a recalcitrant motor was nearly over, and so now maybe crowds weren't so dangerously distracting. As soon as Brookins soloed, in fact, he was to take over the instructorship.[230]

Now that the tensest days of training were over, Orville at last broke his brother's vow not to take passengers and offered a ride to Frank Kohn, the man who had sparked the Montgomery flight venture by donating the land for the training camp in the first place. Well, as Kohn admitted, Wilbur had in jest suggested he would give him an airplane ride—or at least, Kohn had taken such a nearly incredible offer to be a joke, not to be counted on. But here the time had come, and he didn't hesitate. Kohn was the first Montgomerian and no doubt the first Alabamian to go aloft in an airplane. On a beautifully blue and cloudless May 3, he and Orville circled upward over the city, giving Kohn a perspective on Montgomery that no one else who lived in the state capital had ever seen. "It was glorious," Kohn told the *Advertiser*. "It was the most pleasing sensation I have ever experienced." Obviously Kohn had kept up with the ongoing news of engine trouble, because he personally took note of the engine before they took off, ready to scrub the flight if need be. Luckily, the engine purred like it was supposed to, Kohn commented afterward, with some hint of relief.[231]

"The run down the track was like a glide over an ice pond," Kohn explained[232]—though Montgomerians rarely skated on ice ponds. Kohn had grown up in Ohio; he knew about such things.[233] Most Montgomery readers could only imagine what ice skating was like. Realizing this, Kohn tried to make an analogy that his Southern neighbors might understand better. He said, "At express train speed we went over the ground, gradually climbing upward, and the speed, seemingly becoming less." In fact, he and Orville tried to race the Montgomery and Ohio train, but it stopped at camp to let out spectators, so that race was off. Orville asked Kohn if he wanted to go higher, and Kohn said he did. Up they went to a dizzying (for 1910, anyway) three hundred feet. Kohn described the earth gradually falling away. "The sense of motion was lost," he told his fellow Montgomerians. The airplane seemed to stand still.[234]

"The vista then unrolled and was magnificent," Kohn went on, trying hard to put into words the scene that few other Montgomerians were likely to see—at least, no one expected to. By now it was obvious the Wright camp would not be selling regular passenger rides. "For a radius of almost ten miles we could gaze. City, country, hills and vales blended into one pleasing mass of color. And dividing it, as a silver ribbon, flowed the old Alabama [River]."[235]

It was breathtaking, but the airplane had to come down. The aircraft, famous pilot, and honored passenger gradually circled downward. Fifty feet above the ground, Kohn realized how fast the airplane actually was traveling. "It seemed that we were in a runaway automobile," he said. However, he noted, the landing was less jarring than a railroad car stop. Humbled and somewhat overwhelmed by the experience, he felt he could not find adequate words of thanks for the flight.[236]

Kohn found his words later, though. During the flight "came to me the thought of the superiority of the human mind, and of its conquests. One of the things that impressed me during the flight was the sense of security while at the side of Orville Wright," he told the *Advertiser*. "He is the most consummate artist and the greatest mechanic I have ever known, and his machine obeys his lightest touch. I felt in no more danger than I would in a street car."[237] His allusion to Montgomery's other claim to modernity, its streetcars, was well chosen. In Kohn's eyes, the city was journeying into modern times on the wings of progress in transportation.

Orville took up—or tried to take up—other people who had helped with the aviation camp. Thirteen-year-old Earl Kreis had been carrying water out to the unplumbed camp, so he was offered a flight. He reported he was "scared stiff" during the experience.[238] Fred Ball got into the airplane for a flight with Orville, and they slid down the starting rail, when the airplane left the track badly, half jumping the track as it lifted off. The airplane careened to the side, and one of the propellers hit something—Ball never knew what. The propeller went to splinters, and the flight was cancelled. Ball apparently never got his ride.[239]

Following the very high note of Montgomery residents in the air was a very sad, low note indeed. A pilot training camp now being made ready in Dayton was almost completed. Orville would be leaving soon. Brookins would take over the teaching duties in Alabama.[240]

# 5

# THE STUDENTS AND THE
# STUDENT TEACHER

T he news of Orville's imminent departure brought on a throbbing panic in Montgomery. Orville had to deny widespread rumors that the Montgomery camp was going to be abandoned immediately in favor of Dayton. "No, that report is not true," he said emphatically on May 4. "Until the weather in Ohio becomes more favorable for flights, we will maintain both camps. The aviation field in Montgomery will be in operation for several weeks longer, perhaps until the last of this month."[241]

With Brookins now certified, Orville had a pilot to spare to run the Montgomery school. Brookins had at last flown solo—twice in one day, in fact. He showed deft control in the air and was able to take off in less-than-ideal circumstances in a fairly high wind. Even more important, he landed safely. "Well, I'm glad the first flight is over," he said. The *Advertiser* noted that he took congratulations "modestly, as does his teacher."[242] Brookins was likely the first person trained specifically as a flight instructor in the nation, if not the world. He was the first graduate of America's first civilian pilot school, anyway, as well as of the nation's first pilot instructor school.[243]

The key now was time. While it was good news that Brookins had earned his diploma, everyone wanted to see Orville fly, not his student. Hundreds of people swarmed to the aviation field during Orville's last few days there. "Although W. R. Brookins made a number of difficult as well as graceful flights, the crowd would not be satisfied," the *Advertiser* reported on May 6. "Patiently they waited behind the ropes, in the hope of seeing the teacher himself guide his machine." At last Orville flew. The crowd oohed and aahed as he climbed to eight hundred feet and then descended in a long series of dips. Suddenly he made a sharp turn, then glided some more. Forty feet above ground, he rounded the field again before landing. The crowd gave him an ovation.[244]

Alas, the delicate aircraft was damaged by vibrations of the propeller during the flight and had to be taken into the shed for repairs.[245]

It was an anticlimactic ending to a spectacular flight. However, Orville added back the star quality in a move that was completely unexpected. The famous bachelor actually went along with it when a "pretty little Montgomery brunette" approached him, the *Advertiser* said, and "with characteristic politeness and good nature," Orville posed for a picture with her. Then she insisted he have a chocolate, and then that he autograph the chocolate box. The flirtatious young lady went away pleased, anticipating that the autograph would become a treasure. "You know," she said, "I want this signature to

*Orville (center) and students work on the Montgomery airplane.*

show my friends when you are famous and I am old and gray."[246] The fact that one of the world's most eligible bachelors was paired up favorably with a pretty Montgomery lass was probably a cause for excitement in town. Perhaps Orville could be made to stay permanently after all. If flying weather wasn't enough allure, perhaps a pretty girl was!

However, a steady girlfriend for Orville never materialized, and the *Advertiser* avoided any more matchmaking stories. The newspaper turned its attentions to making sure the aviation-crazed public had some way to view the airplane before it flew away for good. Montgomerians who couldn't make it to the airfield wanted to see the Flyer, so the *Advertiser* obliged with a picture that had been taken locally, unlike the earlier ones taken at Fort Myer. This one was a photo of the airplane parked on the ground with Orville and two students working on it. In a humorous mistake, the editor labeled it, "Wright's Aeroplane Climbing Into Cloudland."[247]

Indeed, Orville could trust his students to make repairs without him now. The time had come to turn over the controls to the next generation of pilots. Accordingly the *Advertiser*'s aviation writer did his best to build up Brookins's work as worthy of the master. "It is expected that some fine exhibitions will be given by the new aspirants for honors in aviation, and preparations have been made for large crowds during the next few weeks that the camp is maintained at Montgomery," the newspaper said, trying to keep interest at a high peak.[248]

Orville Wright left town the next day, May 7. After the long, down-in-the-dumps days when the Wrights and their employees had refused to entertain questions from press and public, Orville had by now won over the town. "Orville Wright smiles when he thinks of Montgomery. The smile is friendly and kind, for he has learned to love the city and its people," the *Advertiser* reported with satisfaction. In fact, the article judged that the two months of Orville's stay in Montgomery had been the most productive two months in all his work in aviation[249]—a bit of wishful thinking, given the breakthroughs that took place with the actual first flight in North Carolina and the perfecting of the airplane in Dayton. It seemed Montgomery had won over Orville as well. The great pilot praised Montgomery for its terrific weather. He even hinted, as he left town, that Montgomery could perhaps become a permanent flying center. That remained to be seen, however. Whether Montgomery would gain a long-term flight instruction school "will be determined, in some measure, by the variety of weather which it offers during the winter," Orville said. In a doleful summary of Orville's departure, the *Advertiser* noted that the newly minted Dayton training center would now be the focus of curiosity-seekers' attention.[250]

Montgomerians sadly had to face facts. Orville was really leaving, and thus the city's publicity star was setting. The city could not foresee, however, that the Wright students would do their best to stay in the aviation spotlight, even without their renowned teacher.

The Prince of the Air had hardly flown from Montgomery, when the students showed their capability—and lack thereof. In a hasty landing after a takeoff-gone-wrong due to equipment failure, one of them smashed up the wings of the airplane pretty badly. Brookins, Crane, and Hoxsey, the three Wright men left in camp, set about repairing the wings, a task that they estimated would take four days. Thankfully, attendance was down already, and not that many people saw the accident.[251]

Even in defeat, however, the Wright students looked better than A. Holland Forbes and his partner, J. C. Yates, who were attempting to break the long-distance balloon record in a dirigible. The two were found in the wrecked craft on May 10, unconscious and in critical condition. The dirigible had crashed under mysterious circumstances.[252] When Forbes recovered enough to talk, he revealed some of the dangers of high-altitude flight, the type the Wrights' airplane could not do. The aeronauts had met bitter cold and a snowstorm at 16,000 feet before being shot upward to an estimated 20,600 feet in their virtually uncontrollable craft. The numbed, "half stupid" aeronauts lost their ability to function at the high altitude before Forbes panicked and rushed a descent—a move that did not work. Gravity took care of the rest, though, when at last the gas ran out.[253]

The fresh new aviators in Montgomery didn't look nearly so bad. Even though they had cracked up the airplane, the young Wright pilots made themselves heroes in Montgomery as they awaited yet another airplane part from Dayton. There was nothing much the young trainees and their new teacher could do aviation-wise over the weekend of May 13. Accordingly,

*Commerce on the Alabama River as Brookins and Crane would have seen it on their float to Selma.*

Brookins and Crane decided they'd see Selma, Alabama, traveling there a much more traditional way—by floating down the Alabama River. Friday morning they decided to attempt the adventure and jumped right into it, buying a skiff that very day. They "put out from the foot of Commerce Street on their journey down the muddy waters of the old river," the *Advertiser* reported,[254] harking back to the interesting description by Frank Kohn of the Alabama as a "silver ribbon" as seen from the air. Truly, things looked different from the ground.

Brookins and Crane planned to float downstream until nightfall and then to knock on doors at farmhouses until they found a place to stay for the night. Now very much celebrities, the two no doubt felt they would be welcomed with open arms by the Alabamians who loved watching them work. They expected to get up with the sun on Saturday and "continue their glide down the river to Selma. At Selma they intend to sell the craft and return to Montgomery by railroad," they explained to the now-familiar aviation reporter from the *Advertiser*. The other young pilot, Arch Hoxsey, "was implored, begged and entreated by the other two to make the river trip with them," the newspaper said. Hoxsey refused.[255]

But never mind Hoxsey's reluctance—the three young men had endeared themselves to Montgomery already. "The three young pioneers of the skies speak regretfully of their contemplated departure from Montgomery," commented the newspaper. "One of them, telling Saturday night of the hospitality [and] good fellowship of Montgomery people, said that it will be with a genuine pang that they will leave Montgomery Wednesday."[256]

It seemed much too soon that they would go. "With the coming of the summer, Wright's aeroplane, like all other birds, will fly northward," the *Advertiser* reported poetically, warning readers that there would only be two more days of public flights. The paper reassured its readers that the departure of the aviators was not due to any fault of the city. "The Wright brothers were not impelled by any disadvantage of Montgomery, in deserting the camp here, but because it was considered more advantageous to concentrate the student corps, and to have them all employed at the home camp at Dayton, there to learn the art of aviation," the newspaper said. Estimating that thousands of people had been out to the Montgomery camp to witness flight, the paper added with regret, "One of the showplaces of the city will [be] eliminated with the departure Wednesday."[257]

One report that perhaps interested the student pilots was the *Advertiser's* assertion that the students had never meant to make spectacular flights. As a result, the paper said on May 22, the students were keeping close to the ground.[258] Maybe that statement made the students want to make something spectacular of their work, after all. Other reports of aviation also may have influenced them. Forbes and Yates, the hapless balloonists, had actually achieved a height record in their ill-starred dirigible, sailing to a confirmed 18,000 feet. Even better, the balloonists somehow managed (in their delirious state) to snap "some valuable photographs of the comet"—Halley's Comet, then paying its periodic visit to Earth.[259] The trio of Wright aviators no doubt also saw the news of a balloonist in St. Louis, who tried to explore the tail of Halley's Comet in the aircraft. The balloonist went up at 6:30 PM and stayed up until 11:20 PM, traveling sixty-five miles. The balloon never did get very high, but it did stop at dusk to take on fifty children who had a short flight to see Halley's. Actually, the children's ride was tethered, but the excitement was high anyway. Departing without the children, the balloon nearly crashed onto a freight train. Washington University Professor

*A rear view of the Montgomery airplane. Here the students take charge of the propellers, just as they took charge of the flight school.*

George O. James, head of the balloon expedition, scanned the skies in vain with his telescope, hoping to see traces of Halley's tail.[260]

Whether these events inspired a desire in the Wright students to rise above mundane flight, or whether in typical schoolboy fashion the students misbehaved when the teacher was absent, the young pilots decided to leave their own marks on Montgomery. Spencer Crane left for Dayton, but the remaining pilots, Arch Hoxsey and W. R. Brookins, decided to take some risks. In one event that stretched the airplane and pilots past their known limits, they flew the airplane for more than thirty minutes on May 23, breaking all local flight-time records.[261] It was no small feat, for many flights at the camp had lasted just five minutes, and huge audiences had gathered to witness flights of fifteen minutes and less.[262] The student pilots announced, too, that they intended to fly before sunup. "While the hour may not be popular, the young aviators promise that the event will be picturesque," the *Advertiser* reported.[263] In fact, the young pilots decided to see Halley's Comet from on high,[264] and perhaps they planned to photograph it as Forbes and Yates had, given the comment about the night-hours flight being "picturesque."

Brookins and Hoxsey were getting so good at piloting that the *Adver-*

*tiser*'s now veteran aviation reporter judged their everyday flights to be as entertaining and "as interesting as the flights [of] Orville Wright himself." Their flights, the newspaper said in review, were breaking clear of the classroom stipulations to stay low and keep flights short. "But, gradually learning the knack of buffeting air currents and of guiding the machine, their curves are becoming more picturesque, and their flights more daring," the reporter assessed.[265]

Brookins and Hoxsey weren't joking about plans to fly at night, and the aviation reporter for the *Advertiser* knew it. He stayed up the night of May 25 to see the nation's—if not the world's—first true night airplane flights. The experience left the writer feeling poetic, his powers of description enjoying full play. "A dark, weird, uncertain bulk, glinting now and then in the moonlight as its burnished bars caught the rays, and spouting sparks in mid-air, the aeroplane of the Wright brothers was driven in what is believed to have been the first flights by night ever attempted," he wrote. Besides trying to see Halley's Comet, the "boys," as the *Advertiser* called them, had theorized that winds would die down at night and thus create better flying conditions. They had waited for a good night weather-wise, and May 25 had proved to be the night. As the reporter described it:

> Not a cloud in the sky, the moon shining big and full, and no breeze stirring, the weather was ideal. The first flight was made about 10:30 o'clock, and at regular intervals the flights were continued throughout the night and early morning hours, ten, fifteen to twenty minutes each in duration.
>
> The flying was spectacular. The moon, shining brightly, gave full view of [the] aeroplane, whose dark bulk throbbed through the air, the staccato explosions of the gasoline engine marked by tiny sparks. Now and then the exhaust would scatter a trail of sparks behind the aeroplane in its rapid flight in mid-air.[266]

The silence of the night carried the sound of the engine clearly to the earthbound. For miles away people heard it, even on the outskirts of Montgomery some three miles distant. "In the vicinity of the aviation field, the explosions of the engine were startling with their unwonted noise, and negroes thronged the Washington Ferry Road and peered out cabin windows through the early morning hours," the reporter noticed.[267]

After a twenty-minute flight that ended shortly after midnight, Brookins and Hoxsey declared that night flights were far more satisfactory than day flights, because the air was still. Their theory on calm night winds had been accurate. "There was a thrilling side to the experience," the reporter added, unwittingly touching on realities of future aviation that made blind flying on instruments a must:

> There were no lights on the big field, except that of the moon. Below them, there [were] shadows and indistinctness. Two hundred to three hundred feet high, and little or nothing could be distinguished, just below them. And when the aeroplane left the starting track, as it rose in the air, the experience was that of being hurtled forward, blindly, into the darkness. Guiding was an art. The aviators felt their way through the air currents.[268]

Amazingly enough, the daring young Mr. Hoxsey bested his instructor Brookins by guiding the airplane for his first solo piloting experience on that midnight flight. Brookins's inaugural solo had been more typical, in daytime, of course. Hoxsey and Brookins, the *Advertiser* lauded, were the youngest aviators in the business, but "they established a daring precedent in the field of aerial navigation."[269]

The dangerous but exhilarating midnight flights looked back not so very long ago in time to when Gilbert Edge had drawn a rather pathetic imitation of a biplane in his editorial cartoon, touting the publicity campaign for Montgomery and the South. The airplane had floated in the night sky, casting a beam onto the city. No one had dreamed then that in just four short months, there really would be an airplane above the city on a hitherto unheard-of night flight.

Hoxsey and Brookins stayed up all night, flying in short bursts for twelve hours altogether. Exultant, as the *Advertiser* described them, but also exhausted, they at last returned to their rooms in Montgomery the next

*Walter Brookins, left, and his student, Arch Hoxsey, prepare for a flight; the recently graduated Brookins had taken over the instructorship.*

afternoon and went to bed. "In the hours of travel through the sky" the previous night, the aviation reporter speculated, "the big machine probably was driven farther than any other aeroplane in a similar length of time." The two pilots had alternated taking the controls of the craft all night. They were so happy with their flights that they announced plans to fly at night much more frequently. "The boys are working strenuously, more so than perhaps any other aviator in the history of the art, and are rapidly acquiring the perfection of aviation that has been attained by few men in the world," the *Advertiser* said, amusingly forgetting Wilbur and Orville's strenuous work to discover the principles of flight and to perfect the airplane.[270]

Alas for the history-making night flights in Montgomery, the airplane's motor chain broke on the last flight that day, and rather than send repairs, Orville ordered his students to Dayton, so that they could train to exhibit the airplane in an upcoming aviation meet in Indianapolis. There, in fact, the pilots would debut as the Wright Exhibition Team. Time spent waiting for repair parts in Montgomery when the camp was soon to close was time wasted, as Orville saw it. He telegraphed Brookins and Hoxsey on May 27 to pack up the broken airplane and ship it to Indianapolis.[271]

It was over. Almost as suddenly as Wilbur Wright had appeared in Montgomery in February, all at once there would be no more night flights, no more records in distance traveled aloft, no more aviation tourists pouring into Montgomery. As a footnote to the whole experience, the two young pilots did inform their boss of the altitudes they had achieved in night flight. They thought they had broken altitude records by climbing to 1,500 feet. Orville asked them to measure carefully the height they had attained in the city to substantiate the claim of a record.[272]

Brookins and Hoxsey were heading off to show their skills as daredevils in exhibitions, fairs, and aviation meets.[273] They hadn't been trained as daredevils, but the skills learned in Montgomery gave them courage to try death-defying stunts. Despite that exciting future, they were already nostalgic for their old flying school days. "The young men were not jubilant at leaving Montgomery. Rather they were disheartened, for they said Saturday that there will always be a warm spot in their hearts for Montgomery and gratitude for their reception here," the *Advertiser* sighed. "Aviation days are over for Montgomery, at least until aviation becomes a more familiar pastime." Meanwhile, the Kohn place looked awfully forlorn. "Except the wooden shed, covered with glaring advertisements, there is nothing there to identify the Kohn plantation with the advent of the Wright brothers," the newspaper said.[274]

At last it was time to sum up the work of the Wrights in Montgomery. The *Advertiser*'s faithful and seasoned aviation reporter sharpened his quill with his most poetic and sentimental work yet. Not only did he offer a good summation of Wright achievements in Montgomery, but he put aviation of the day in perspective:

The establishment of the training camp in Montgomery marks the beginning of an epoch in aviation. It was proof that aviation had made good, and that it was an established science to be imparted by rule to others . . .

The establishment of the camp in Montgomery reveals a new profession, also for young men, for daring resourceful young men. The word "aviator" has become, all over the world, the "open sesame" to dreams of a dazzling new vocation since Wilbur Wright first came to Montgomery, unheralded and unexpected, four months ago.

To the superficial observer . . . there was nothing of significance accomplished at the camp on the Washington Ferry Road. But below the surface there was much work done. First of all, there [were] created five new aviators, and when the entire world's supply of aviators can be counted on the fingers, the augmentation of the supply is significant . . . It was left to the young new aviators themselves, with their daring of enthusiasm, to make the first real flights by night in the history of aviation. Heretofore there has been no flying after dark.

Paulhan, for instance, in his notable flight in Great Britain, effected a portion of his journey after dusk had fallen. But never, until two boys in Montgomery, Alabama, new to the art of aviation, drove their machine in impressive flights through the dark skies for hours, were the night hours chosen for aerial navigation.[275]

The *Advertiser*'s assessment of aviation in mid-1910 was correct. Aviation was the wave of the future, but the wave at that moment belonged mainly to a very few daring young men. Having observed aviation more closely than any other reporter in America for the past four months, the *Advertiser*'s writer struggled now, at the end of the camp, to describe what made an aviator. An aviator, he said, "must be, above all, daring, and possessing what Americans call 'nerve,' that quality of fearlessness and pluck which most men love to think that they possess. And with that nerve, there must be the ability to apply it instantaneously. The air is no element for the dullard or the slow-thinker." An airman, he said, had to think as fast as

*Orville Wright and his tie-wearing Montgomery students pose by the airplane. The Wrights expected their pilots to be clean and well-dressed.*

the wind, literally, in order to counteract the wind "or be dashed to death." But these, as the reporter mused, were also qualities in the ordinary driver of automobiles, and surely, he felt, aviators had to have more. There were lots of aspects to be considered—the Wrights had chosen their students for their high morals and good hygiene, for example. The young men did not have bad habits; in fact, the young men were like athletes. Yes, that was it—what really set aviators apart. The reporter latched onto the common idea of the day that airplane operators were, at heart, sportsmen.[276] Thousands of spectators had turned out in Montgomery with that very sense that they were watching some breathtaking sports event. Aviation in mid-1910 was still a sport, mainly meaningful to the ordinary non-participant as something to be ogled and cheered.

Nearly two months before, Orville had suggested that potential pilots needed a good understanding of mechanics. By now, however, the *Advertiser* recognized that a mechanic did not necessarily make a pilot—in fact, a pilot should actually be able to tune out the sounds of motors and pistons. Presumably a mechanic would be disturbed by every little clang—and the Montgomery spectators of the past few months knew quite well that little clangs seemed to happen on every flight. Thus, a pilot would probably do well *not* to be a mechanic. One thing an aviator did need, however, the *Advertiser* declared, was a "knowledge of higher and more intricate mathematics," useful for bringing theories into the realm of reality.[277] The revised assessment of a pilot's job qualifications was sophisticated, given the simpler ideal before of a daring mechanic. Indeed, America's first civilian flight school was teaching the world about who should and could pilot airplanes—an essential feature to making aviation an ongoing success and not just a momentary phenomenon isolated to the Wright brothers and other first-generation pilots.

Also revised was the *Advertiser*'s assessment of Montgomery in the recounting of the Wright camp's achievements. While the Wrights were in Montgomery, the aviation reporter said, "the average Montgomerian lost sight of the fact that the pioneers of the sky were here for business, simply, and the romantic glamour with which Montgomery people invested their work here had entered in no way into their plans."[278] Indeed, the *Advertiser*'s early jealousy of the Wright camp's reticence had melted away, as it pretty much had to. The great flyers were there for work, and in the long run the city wanted to be part of that vital work, not a hindrance to it, even if questions went unanswered and would-be spectators went away dissatisfied at times. As the reporter summed it up:

> In Montgomery the aviators were not at play; they were not on exhibition. Here, perhaps more than at any other time in its history, did aviators descend to prosaic toil and actual labor. Orville Wright and his students were not here, primarily for tests or experiments. They came after tests and experiments had been worked out, and they were here for the application of the results.[279]

The honest description of the down-and-dirty Wright work extended to the final analysis of Montgomery's role as well. Whereas the city at first had basked in a flirtatious glow that came from courting the Princes of the Air, Montgomery at last realized it had not been romanced as the beautiful princess. The Wright-Montgomery alliance had been a marriage of convenience—happy in the long run, but not a real love match.

Of course, there had been a great deal of infatuation on the part of local citizens. Montgomerians had fallen so hard for the aviators that city residents had actually skipped the season's baseball games in noticeable numbers as they hurried to the Wright camp to see the airplane fly. But in general only the spectators watching the Wrights had stars in their eyes. The Wrights themselves did not. As the now wiser *Advertiser* admitted at last, "Montgomery was selected by the Wrights in the same business-like way that characterized their plans throughout. It was not chosen with any view to beauty, or hospitality of population, but after weather maps and records had been perused, and Montgomery was selected because of its universally [warm] temperatures and lack of high wind."[280]

One of Montgomery's important goals had been achieved, though, and that was good publicity for the South. The *Advertiser* singled out that fact. Four months before, Gilbert Edge had drawn the little-understood biplane, floating in the night sky, casting a beacon down upon Montgomery in a publicity campaign billing the South as "The Young Man's Opportunity." The beam of fine publicity in the cartoon had fallen from the airplane through the night to Montgomery, but its radiance had illuminated the entire region. Perhaps the aviation writer for the *Advertiser* had that on his mind when he reckoned up the Wrights' work for the South as a whole. "The establishment of the camp in Montgomery brought the South into the world's eye as identified with the last work in human progress, the control of the air," he said in a summary that would have pleased Mr. Trezevant of New Orleans' Progressive Union. "The Southern states, in line with every other modern event and improvement, assured the world of [their] development through Montgomery's association with aviation. That is the most significant thing."[281]

Perhaps it really was the most significant thing. The future was now; the Civil War was past. Symbolic of the pre-Civil War plantation system crumbling into the future, the Kohn cotton plantation had been transformed into the nation's first civilian flying school, and most of the witnesses to the first night flights had been black field hands, not whites. The future had come to the Deep South, and the Wright brothers had brought it with them.

In one final statement, the *Advertiser's* anonymous reporter hung up his illustrious aviation beat with a sad sentence: "The aviation days of Montgomery are over, for a great while."[282]

Even stubborn editor Screws, who had groused so frequently about aviation and had been so dubious about the Wrights on general principles, came around as the aviation camp broke up. "Of course America had to lead in aviation. We could not afford to have any effete European government even claiming supremacy," he commented, thumbing his nose at the Frenchman Paulhan, who had been grabbing headlines for his London-to-Manchester flight and for planning a London-to-Paris flight. "In all ages it will be known that two Americans, the Wright brothers, first mastered the marvellous art of flying through the atmosphere on a heavier than air machine. Since [the Wright brothers] there have been many mono-planes, bi-planes and others of the flying machine craft, but they were built upon the principle that two Americans discovered."[283] And of course, although it was not spoken in the editorial, Montgomery had had an important role in America's ongoing air supremacy. Montgomery was the center of flight for those precious few months, and the city had produced a few of the handful of qualified pilots in the nation, soon to take on Paulhan for other records.[284]

It was amusing that Screws—so recently curmudgeonly in all things involving aviation—was ready to stick up for the city's heroic flight professor and brother. In a week that saw Glenn Curtiss make a heralded flight between New York City and Albany[285] and Charles Stewart Rolls (of Rolls-Royce fame) fly across the English Channel and back without stopping,[286] the editor suddenly had a sentimental desire to embroider the Wright image. "The long flights of aviators in the last few days are drawing a lot of attention," Screws wrote, "but it is safe to say the public will see the 'real thing' when one of the Wright brothers goes out on a long distance spin." He then took off on a tongue-in-cheek flight of fancy:

It would not surprise Montgomery people, after what they have seen at the practice camp, for one of the aviators to skim back to Montgomery after a propeller blade, a chisel, or some other article that may have been forgotten when they moved. During the course of the flights here the machine seemed perfectly under control, and if it can do all the manouvering it went through in mere "school" work, it has wonders stored in its make-up for a long distance flight. Save the big hurrah until one of the Wrights tries for distance.[287]

Now the Wrights became far-off news for Montgomery readers. In a front-page story that had perhaps precipitated the editor's bluster over the Wrights' potential long-distance record, Orville announced from Ohio on June 2 that his team would enter all long-distance flying races in the upcoming Indianapolis air meet.[288] Perhaps the recent flights in Montgomery gave him confidence in victory. Also, Montgomery readers learned, Charles Stewart Rolls made his nonstop, round-trip flight across the English Channel in a Wright biplane. French flyer Louis Bleriot had been the first to conquer the English Channel, and the French Count Jacques de Lesseps had followed in his wake, but "it remained for an Englishman in an American machine to perform the double feat," the Associated Press bragged.[289]

The Wrights and their students at last commanded the front page of the *Advertiser*, which they had never done during their stay in Montgomery, the front being reserved for Associated Press stories and local tales of dire tragedy. Now that the Wrights were gone, the Associated Press was feeding stories of them to page one of the *Advertiser*. The lead story of June 13 announced that the Wright brothers had entered six biplanes in the Indianapolis air show, and Wilbur had gone to Indianapolis to supervise.[290]

The Wright work in Alabama certainly paid off in the Indianapolis meet as the Montgomery pupils showed what they had learned. The star student from Montgomery, W. R. Brookins, flew his Wright biplane to a height of 4,384.5 feet in Indianapolis, which broke the world's record for airplane altitude. In fact, he took the record from the great Paulhan, who had achieved 4,165 feet not so long ago in Los Angeles. The Associated Press report described a Brookins who duplicated the flying techniques he had perfected in Montgomery, rising higher and higher in easy circles until the crowd could hear his machine no more. Both of the Wrights were there to cheer their star pupil, and so did the spectators as Brookins stepped out of his airplane upon landing. A tagline at the end of the Associated Press piece threw a little pride back toward Montgomery. "W. R. Brookins, who broke all records for altitude at the aviation meet in Indianapolis," the article read, "is the first pupil who was trained by Orville Wright at the spring training camp on the Washington Ferry Road, near Montgomery. Upon the departure of Mr. Wright for Dayton, O., Mr. Brookins was left in charge of the camp." Arch Hoxsey, the article added, also entered events in Indianapolis. The two "established a record in Montgomery by making midnight flights," the article reminded proud Montgomerians as they followed their favorite sons' feats.[291]

The same day that Brookins grabbed headlines for high flying, Charles K. Hamilton illustrated other impressive directions for airplanes. Hamilton finished a flight from New York to Philadelphia, an American cross-country record. He accomplished the trip in one hour and fifty-one minutes and covered eighty-eight miles, although Hamilton had to stop once on his way back due to a sluggish motor. Hamilton delivered some air mail from various New York dignitaries to their counterparts in Philadelphia—the first air mail, the Associated Press said, touting the newly realized fact that mail could be delivered efficiently and on time via airplane.[292] Shortly Hamilton announced he would enter a contest to fly from Chicago to New York. "There isn't any doubt about the feasibility of such a trip," he told the press.[293] He also announced he would enter a New York to St. Louis race, seeking a $30,000 prize.[294]

Meanwhile, as the Indianapolis airplane meet continued over the next few days, Brookins had an anticlimactic ending to his record-breaking heroics. He tried to best his own altitude record and thought he had done it when his instruments showed he had reached 5,000 feet. However, the aneroid barometer was not in working order, and it turned out he only had reached 3,700 feet.[295] Brookins's years-later recounting of his flight that broke the record at the Indianapolis meet illustrated just how steely the nerves of pilots of 1910 really were:

> I took off, with flying conditions about perfect, and started to climb. By the way, I climbed at the rate of about 70 feet a minute as compared to 700 for a good ship today. More or less to my surprise everything went well. I struck no strong winds and the air was pretty firm.
>
> I intended to keep on going up until I reached the climbing limit of the motor. And then it happened. At first, from the noise, I thought the motor was tearing itself loose from the ship. As a matter of fact, a valve had broken, shifted out over the top of its piston, and on the

next upstroke pushed the whole top of the cylinder off. There I was, up 4,200 feet with a dead motor. I had broken the altitude record, and if my luck held, I'd break the gliding record too. If it didn't, I'd probably break my neck. It held. I came down in a very wide spiral, nosed into the field and landed without the least trouble.[296]

Arch Hoxsey also had a hard time in Indianapolis. His Wright airplane cut out at eight hundred feet, and it fell into a steep dive. Hoxsey was able to regain control and landed in a neighboring field.[297] After that, the Wrights and their team packed up for another aviation meet in Montreal.[298]

Orville Wright and his students had left Montgomery to perform in Indianapolis, and by June 18, even Indianapolis was over. Aviation was truly no more in Montgomery, Alabama.

*The Class of 1910, posing in Montgomery. From left, Arthur L. Welsh, Spencer M. Crane, Orville Wright, Walter R. Brookins, James Davis, and Archibald Hoxsey.*

# 6

# WHATEVER HAPPENED
# TO THE CLASS OF 1910?

After the weeks of the Wright brothers' Montgomery flying school, the world was a wiser place aviation-wise, having gained not only more pilots but also a keener knowledge among aviators of how to teach flight. The class of 1910 at the Alabama flying school included two newly qualified pilots, W. R. Brookins and Arch Hoxsey; Arthur Welsh, who became a pilot soon afterward in Dayton; James Davis, who never quite graduated but became an airplane mechanic, and one dropout, Spencer Crane. But there were more than those graduates and near-graduates who counted the flight school as a great course in things hitherto unknown. Orville, for one, researched how to teach pilots, a very new skill that he or others could replicate in other settings, a key component of all good professional research. The city of Montgomery, by the end of the semester, not only had passed its crash course in aviation but also had developed its own vision of the future. Apparently much of the world now knew more of Montgomery as well—the city had graduated from anonymity and had concurrently redirected thought about the South away from the ashes of history and, it was hoped, into the future.

Montgomery's press graduated much wiser, too, as recorders of early flight. As the Wright camp dwindled and then departed, it became obvious that the *Advertiser*, once so ignorant of flight, momentarily led the media world in understanding and coverage of aviation. In January and February, editorial cartoonist Gilbert Edge had enthusiastically if faultily splashed biplanes throughout his futuristic pictures. With the coming of the Wright aviation school, though, Edge had had a long time to study the look and operation of airplanes. He was now an expert. His May 11 "Howdy!" cartoon showed the outstretched hand of Montgomery reaching toward a woman and two men. The woman represented the Daughters of the Confederacy, while the men represented the Fire Underwriters of Alabama and the Opticians of

HOWDY!

*At last cartoonist Gilbert Edge drew a perfect biplane. He was one of the few cartoonists in the world who had actually seen an airplane, and the improvement in his depiction of it was obvious.*

Alabama (that figure sported a thick pair of glasses). All of the groups were convening in Alabama's capital. Edge threw in a beautifully drawn biplane overhead—Montgomery's claim to fame above all.[299] The accurate, gracefully depicted biplane was a dramatic improvement in Edge's cartooning work on the subject of aviation. He was now an eyewitness to flight, one of the few cartoonists with such an advantage, and it showed.

The staff writers had also grown enlightened on the subject of flight. While the *Advertiser* had fallen hard for the Birmingham birdman who claimed to have flown secret night flights all over town and to have been spotted by residents of Woodlawn, the *Advertiser* now recognized that he was a fraud. The newspaper realized rightfully that airplane flights drew far too much attention to be kept that much a secret. Thus, the *Advertiser* now credited Brookins and Hoxsey in Montgomery with the first night flights in history.

For Montgomery residents, the short course in the airplane of 1910 developed into an ongoing continuing education course in a subject most other Americans were not nearly so well schooled in. As Louis Paulhan made headlines for planning a flight from London to Paris, the *Advertiser* designed quite a spread to help explain the would-be feat to eager subscribers, incorporating maps, a photo of the great pilot, a photo of his airplane, and a photo of the Eiffel Tower.[300] Montgomery readers, now among the savviest airplane enthusiasts in the world, found their attention drawn to Paris, and their understanding of Paulhan's heroics sharpened. Certainly flying a biplane like Paulhan's a total of 259 miles between capitals was staggering—an amazing thing—but to Montgomerians, more so than to most Americans, the Frenchman's plan was comprehensible.

Paulhan's flight would take him across the English Channel, of course. But truthfully, Channel crossings were starting to lose their novelty. Before Paulhan, Charles Rolls had won the prize as the first pilot to fly across the Channel and back without stopping. Before Rolls, Count de Lesseps had successfully completed one leg of the cross-channel round-trip before being forced down by fog in his Bleriot monoplane.[301] And before de Lesseps, Louis Bleriot had first crossed the Channel by air. After de Lesseps, *Advertiser* editor Screws quipped, "Only three Frenchmen have ever successfully crossed the English Channel, with their minds on high things. They were Louis Bleriot, the Count DeLesseps and one who crossed a long time ago—Duke William of Normandy."[302] In a more serious comment on the crossing of the Channel by airplane, Screws showed the incisive thinking that resulted from a thorough schooling on the subject of aviation. He said:

> A second Frenchman, flying through the air has overtopped Eng-
> land's "wall of water" and dropped unheralded on her soil. England
> is startled. Is "the wall of water" to be no longer a protection to the
> tight little isle? All that saved England from an invasion by the armies
> of Napoleon were the victories of the English over the inefficient navy
> of Napoleon's admirals.

Astutely, the editor drew conclusions about the grimmer prospects of flight, now having been perfected to a greater degree in Montgomery itself: "What protection is the wall of water, what protection is England's magnificent navy, if man-birds can sail 2,000 feet above them and drop upon English soil?" He added a sober final note, something of a warning to England from his vantage point as an aviation insider in Montgomery: "And England is behind every first class power in the development of flying machines."[303]

All the *au courant* aviation news wasn't quite as impressive as the potential invasion of England. Chauvetto Michelin, a French aviator, was killed during a race in Lyons, France, after his airplane struck a telephone booth.[304] In Joplin, Missouri, J. C. Mars's airplane caused panic at an air show when it went out of control, veering toward the bleachers. The flyer pulled the plane out of its dive less than a foot over the head of terrified onlookers, and several people suffered minor injuries in the panic.[305] Ten-year-old Freddie Meyers of Chillicothe, Ohio, was whisked skyward when a dirigible he was exploring broke free of its moorings, carrying the boy five miles away while thousands watched in horror. The gas in the balloon was gradually depleted, and the terrified lad jumped safely when the dirigible sank to within ten feet of the ground. Without Freddie's weight, the craft shot upward and disappeared.[306] Indeed, as Wilbur had said so long ago in Montgomery, dirigibles just didn't make trustworthy aircraft.

Not that everyone had given up entirely on dirigibles, by any means. The fashion industry deemed the dirigible both safe and forward-thinking as it created the "dirigible gown" of 1910. The garment was meant to replace the immodest fashion fad of pantaloons, which women just didn't want to give up. Pantaloons were, after all, comfortable and serviceable, and the dirigible gown was designed to serve the needs of both comfort and modesty. This newest fashion development looked like a walking gown but could be changed with a few buttonings into a garment of ease for women who wished to do forward-thinking things such as golfing or riding horses. In fact, this clever gown actually was designed for use by women in airplanes[307]—a bonus in an era when the occasional female airplane passenger was compelled to tie her skirts closed against the wind.[308] As to why the garment was not called an "aeroplane gown," it is likely that consumers of 1910—at least, unenlightened ones outside of aviation-savvy places such as Montgomery—still thought that dirigibles were the aeronautic craft of the future. In the case of the ladies, at least the dirigible's proponents looked forward to a time of luxury-filled, fully enclosed passenger compartments, where skirts wouldn't fly. That concept was as yet untried in an airplane, and so perhaps dirigibles seemed more civilized. The *Advertiser*, in fact, reprinted an article from *Century* magazine that predicted what a Zeppelin dirigible would look like in ten years. The airship would hold 125 to 150 passengers and would feature sleeping compartments, a barber shop, a lounge, a reading room, and a fancy dining room. Cooking would be done by electricity. The Zeppelin would make a swift trip across the Atlantic, and to lighten the load, the pampered passengers would bring along only small carry-on bags, their major luggage going by surface ship. The airship would fly along at a clip of 75 to 120 miles per hour.[309]

Of course, readers in Montgomery knew the aviation ropes better than most. They may or may not have bought the message of futuristic luxury in the dirigible story, but they were already seeing that Montgomery's aviation experiments had blazed a path that other aviators were following. In a sense, then, pilots other than Brookins, Hoxsey, and Welsh gained from the 1910 flight school by copying what had been proven there. In early June, for example, an English army airship flew over London itself in the middle of the night. The airplane left its base at 11:30 P.M. and arrived at St. Paul's Cathedral at 1:30 A.M., returning to its base at 3 A.M.[310] That sort of night flight news was startling in a place like London, but it was old hat in Montgomery.

Meanwhile, the now in-the-know editor of the *Advertiser* had some choice words for U.S. Secretary of State Philander Chase Knox, who proposed to have airships registered, just as seagoing vessels were registered. Under Knox's proposal, aircraft would have to get clearance credentials at the customs house in various cities. Apparently the secretary's plan rested on the persistent worry that airplanes could easily be used by criminals. Wilbur Wright had put that fear to rest in Montgomery in an interview with the *Advertiser*, so editor Screws said sarcastically, "This is most wise in the secretary. If the step were not taken no end of diamond smuggling could go on by means of bi-planes, monoplanes, and, in the course of development, who knows but octo-planes may figure." Now, he scoffed, airplanes would have to land at the customs houses, none of which had been built with enough room or on the right terrain for airplanes to take off or land. The editor went on, "With this law enforced it will be impossible for [criminals] to light in the open country beyond a city where a confederate may be waiting." Then he moved in for the kill:

> Smugglers have such great respect for the law they would never think of doing anything so mean. The new law will fix things so that all persons who want good, close views of aviators and their machines will have only to go to the nearest customs house, sit patiently on the steps a week or two, or possibly a month, and then z-z-z-z-zip! There are airship and aviator, waiting to be seen.[311]

It was sarcasm spoken from a Montgomerian's point of view. Airplanes were so few in number and, in Screws's eyes, so doubtful as to their usefulness to criminals that he couldn't perceive of a need for such regulation. Screws could not possibly foresee that Knox's suggestion prefigured airports. To the editor, himself a graduate of the Wright experience, it just sounded ludicrous that smugglers could fly without attracting a staggering number of eager eyewitnesses, just as the Wright airplane had attracted thousands of witnesses in Montgomery. There was also that serious question of how much a criminal could actually smuggle on an open wing with no cargo hold.

Some of the continuing education on aviation after the Wrights' school in Alabama closed tended toward the bizarre. In an *Advertiser* story that in later years might call out alien-hunters, residents of Springfield, Ohio, on the way home from church saw "some great air craft carrying a bright red light" very, very far above the earth and making fast speed. Despite the distance, the whir of the engine was audible. In those more innocent times, the churchgoers assumed the machine was something they had heard about but never seen—a Wright airplane. Orville, however, knew nothing about it when questioned.[312] Then there was the sportsman W. Starling Burgess, who had gone in with Augustus M. Herring to build a new type of biplane that circumvented Wright patents with a curious-looking series of fins attached to the top wing. The device, as pictured on the sports page (pilots were sportsmen, of course), no doubt looked weird to the readers in Montgomery, who

*Burgess Thinks He Has Conquered The Air*

*Sportsman W. Starling Burgess and Augustus M. Herring (inset) tried to beat Wright patents with a series of fins atop the wing of their airplane.*

knew far better than most what an airplane should look like. The sail-like fins were meant to keep the machine from tipping and were expected, as Burgess said, "to correct many of the present evils of flying."[313] It was probably no surprise to those who had watched Orville, Brookins, and Hoxsey fly in Montgomery that the fins never caught on, no doubt because they did not work. In another bizarre report, the *Advertiser* noted that armies of the world were experimenting with an ancient sort of air vessel—they were sending men aloft on gigantic kites, where soldiers took photos of enemy territory below. In fact, the practice of aerial photography was already in use in balloons.[314] Shortly that role would be taken over by airplanes, once again bringing Montgomery into focus in the world of aviation.[315]

But until then, Montgomerians and Alabamians could only fly vicariously through newspaper reports about the Wrights and such birdmen as Wright rival Glenn Curtiss, who won $10,000 for flying from Albany to New York City. The Associated Press reported thousands of cheering crowds for Curtiss's flight, which was being called "the greatest single feat in the history of aviation,"[316] a distinction that Wright fans certainly disagreed with. Nevertheless, the *Advertiser* gave Curtiss a fancy spread, with an artfully designed page depicting Curtiss, his airplane, and a map of his route.[317]

The layout and press attention were worthy of the Montgomery readership. Having been through the 1910 flight school as supporters and spectators, many Alabama residents now truly did perceive of aviation as the future. The theme of the airplane and the future popped up in the activities of students in schools other than Orville's. In a front-page story, the *Advertiser* crowed about Harvard students who had built an airplane of their own. Taking the opposite route of Orville's master-apprentice pilot school, the Harvard men were learning about airplanes and flight theory in the classroom from "skilled professors" and by experimentation.[318]

One of the Harvard students studying aviation was H. S. Ford, class of 1910, from Troy, Alabama, not so very far from Montgomery. Ford and his fellow students were building their own airplane—quite a popular college pursuit, it turned out, since students at Harvard, Yale, Amherst, Columbia, and MIT were all building airplanes. Ford was a charter member of the largest of these student groups, the Harvard Aeronautical Society. The young aeronauts had copied Wright and Bleriot designs. Somehow the young men were allowed to use patented technology—at least, that's what the *Advertiser* said. In reality, all the students had been able to complete so far was a very primitive glider—one that certainly did not make use of the Wrights' patented wing-warping for control in turns. The student-built glider was controlled by the pilot's dangling legs, which he swung right, left, forward, or back to urge the aircraft in the right direction. Even the enthusiastic special report on the project had to admit, "It was a weird sight to see a young man kicking his legs and swinging his body back and forth from between two huge wings."[319]

Even closer to home, fourteen cadets in the Starke University School in Montgomery vied for the Holtzclaw medal, in which the students were given a Saturday morning to write an extemporaneous essay. The subject? Aviation, of course. It would have been a shame not to address such a forward-thinking, localized topic that would also test how well the students had kept their eye on local news events. The benefactor who gave the annual prize selected the topic herself.[320]

Meanwhile, in nearby Birmingham, the *Age-Herald* declared graduation for aviation as a whole. Experimentation had ended, as far as the *Age-Herald* was concerned, with the Montgomery flight school. "Victory Over Air is Now Achieved," the newspaper proclaimed in a headline. The *Age-Herald* quoted Orville, as the *Advertiser* had, suggesting that airplanes would one day carry mail and would take on passenger traffic whenever demand was high enough. Despite the newspaper's confidence, the contradictory statements of other great aviators in the *Age-Herald* article mainly showed that confusion, not conquest, was the actual aura around aviation. Glen Curtiss suggested the airplane would be a weapon of defense, although he felt that a dozen airplanes, working together, could "annihilate" a fleet of battleships[321]—a situation that came true some three decades later on a date which would live in infamy. Louis Paulhan also saw the airplane as a weapon of war, while Baron de Constant thought airplanes would establish peace by "making war impossible." Clifford B. Harmon agreed, foreseeing a time when the world would cease building warships. "Scouting by aeroplanes will swoop away the whole basis of modern warfare. It will make strategy impossible for strategy depends upon secrecy," he said. A more realistic Thomas S. Baldwin predicted that airplanes would one day carry "a ton of mail" and would cross the Atlantic Ocean at speeds of one hundred miles per hour.[322]

Some of the aviators' predictions of the future were accurately prophetic. Airplanes do travel at speeds unthinkable in 1910, and they do cross oceans and carry tons of mail. They transport passengers and are weapons of defense. Sadly, they did not eliminate war, a dream that was shattered shortly in World War I when airplanes began trying their wings in battle. That conflict turned out to be a training ground for military aviation as world leaders began to discern ever more clearly a pivotal career for airplanes in wars of the future. Another sad truth about airplanes voiced often in the Wrights' day was the fact that criminals could use airplanes in the commission of crimes, from smuggling (as had been worried about in 1910) to worse, as anyone could attest after hijacked civilian jetliners smashed into the World Trade Center and the Pentagon on September 11, 2001. The 2001 terror-ist airplane attacks were carried out by student pilots from American flight schools—heirs (although criminal ones) of Hoxsey and Brookins at the first civilian flight school in America.

But in 1910 as the Wright school came to a close in Montgomery, the future looked very bright for aviation and for the eager pilots who had completed the course of study. In October 1910, Arch Hoxsey took up former president Teddy Roosevelt, the first American president (or, at least, ex-president) to experience an airplane flight. Prior to the days of Air Force One, this was a terrifying thing for people who happened to witness the event. No doubt some of the frightened spectators watching Roosevelt's flight had heard that Hoxsey had crashed his airplane into the grandstand at a Milwaukee, Wisconsin, air show the month before, injuring several onlookers.[323] Such news didn't do much for onlookers' confidence in Hox-sey as a pilot. The press framed Roosevelt's adventure as another brave and dangerous move by the famed former president. As the United Press wire service reported the ex-Rough Rider's flight, which took place in St. Louis, "Col. Roosevelt defied death late yesterday when he went up in an aeroplane with aviator Arch Hoxsey. More than 10,000 persons breathlessly watched the flight, fearing the colonel's daring on the spur of the moment might mean his death or injury."[324]

Roosevelt, for his part, loved the three-mile ride. "It was fine. Fine!" he told United Press. Hoxsey admitted that Roosevelt was a bit of a rough rider as a passenger. The former president leaned over the side of the aircraft, waving at the crowd—something even daredevil Hoxsey thought was a little dangerous.

The trip had been entirely unplanned. Roosevelt, upon being introduced to Hoxsey, admitted he was jealous of the airman's accomplishments. "Here's your chance," Hoxsey replied in something of a dare. Roosevelt eagerly took the dare. Hoxsey had to warn his well-known passenger about various safety issues. "Be careful not to pull any of those strings," Hoxsey cautioned the ex-president. "Nothing doing," Roosevelt shouted over the motor, flashing his trademark toothy grin.

Suddenly Hoxsey realized what he had just undertaken. "I said to myself, 'If anything happens to him I'll never be able to square myself with the American people.' . . . I never felt a greater responsibility in my life." Hoxsey might not have worried so much had he not let his daredevil instincts take over. With Hoxsey at the controls, the plane climbed sharply and then dove sharply, hurtling close enough to the ground to cause spectators to gasp. Hoxsey repeated the maneuver several gasp-inducing times. It was a thrill, no doubt, but also a risk with so presidential a passenger.

*Daredevil Montgomery graduate Arch Hoxsey took Teddy Roosevelt on an impromptu airplane flight in St. Louis. Hoxsey professed to be cautious to assure the ex-president's safety, but a newsreel shows that he dove steeply multiple times. Roosevelt thought the flight was "bully." The scratchy stills here come from the newsreel.*

In the air, the former commander-in-chief said something enticing to Hoxsey and anyone else interested in the ongoing debate about the airplane's potential role in war. Unfortunately, Hoxsey couldn't quite make it out. "I heard him say 'war,' 'army,' 'aeroplane' and 'bomb,' but the noise was so great that I could not hear the rest," Hoxsey recounted to the UP reporter.

For his part, Roosevelt summed up the experience in a characteristic thank you to Hoxsey: "That was the bulliest experience I ever had."

Although Hoxsey was nervous about taking up a presidential passenger, little else ruffled him. Hoxsey and Brookins became famous as daredevil exhibition pilots. Brookins was known for his short turns, as well as close-to-ground flying with his wings daringly angled. Hoxsey gained notoriety for "The Dive of Death"—a circling glide followed by a steep dive from 1,000 feet.[325] After Hoxsey had an accident while attempting a showy maneuver at an air meet, Wilbur sent him a stern letter:

> I am very much in earnest when I say that I want no stunts and spectacular frills put on flights [at the next exhibition]. If each of you can make a plain flight of ten to fifteen minutes each day keeping always within the inner fence wall away from the grandstand and never more than three hundred feet high it will be just what we want. Anything beyond plain flying will be chalked up as a fault and not as a credit.[326]

Wilbur's letter might have been describing any ordinary day at the Montgomery training camp, where flights typically ran from ten to fifteen minutes and often stayed under three hundred feet. Such "plain flying" had attracted thousands of visitors to Montgomery, so to Wilbur it seemed natural that crowds would still thrill at the sight of a safe flight. To the Wrights, the imitation of Montgomery was good enough. To the enthusiastic new pilots, however, Wilbur's rules were far too humdrum.

The young pilots defied Wilbur's request for Montgomery-like "plain flying." They couldn't bring themselves to reign in their show when crowds arrived expecting to see daredevil stunts. Sadly, however, such derring-do killed Montgomery darling Arch Hoxsey, who did not survive the year after his pilot training. On the last day of 1910, Hoxsey decided to try to beat the newly set record of 362.66 miles in one sustained flight, achieved only the day before by Maurice Tabuteau, a Frenchman. At stake was a $4,000 prize. Hoxsey took off during a Los Angeles air show, flying around over the crowd, and after an hour also tried to beat the altitude record, which he owned, having set it at 11,474 feet just a week and a half before. This time, though, something went wrong. The *New York American* described the tragedy poignantly:

> He started down in a spiral descent. As the little speck gradually grew larger, it could be seen that the daredevil birdman was rushing earthward with one perpendicular swirl after another. At times it seemed as if the craft almost stood on beam end. Even those who had watched him day after day grew afraid. The cheering subsided to a silent prayer for the man in the frail thing of cloth and sticks.
>
> Suddenly, after he had made a waltzing turn around the purlieus of the field, 500 feet up in the air, he attempted another hair-raising bank. But as the craft almost stood on its end, an unexpected puff of gusty wind blew full blast in its rear. Instantly the craft turned over. The cracking of the spars and ripping of the cloth could be heard as the machine, a shapeless mass, came hurtling to the ground in a series of somersaults.
>
> When the attendants rushed to the tangled mass of wreckage they found the body crushed out of all semblance to a human being. The crowd waited until the announcer megaphoned the fatal news and then turned homeward. All flying was over for the day.[327]

Brookins, by now a close friend of Hoxsey, reportedly broke down and wept at the scene.[328] He was not alone in his feelings. Reflecting widespread public grief at the loss of Hoxsey, Mecca Cigarettes issued a trading card—something like a baseball card—of Hoxsey as part of its "Series of Champion Athletes."[329] With Hoxsey's tragic crash and several others, it was no wonder that the Wright Exhibition Company dissolved just a year and a half after it had made its first flights in Indianapolis.[330]

As to the other young Montgomery pilots, Spencer Crane quit the fly-ing lessons, and James Davis never successfully completed his pilot train-ing. He did stay on, however, as a handyman with the Wright Exhibition Team. As such, he was around Hoxsey and Brookins pretty continually. Davis was probably the unidentified mechanic who used an iron pipe to fend off souvenir hunters who tried to take away mementos after Hoxsey's fatal crash.[331]

Montgomery student Arthur Welsh soon finished the pilot's course he had started in Alabama. He succeeded in becoming a pilot instructor in Dayton, but he, too, met with a tragic end. After the Wright Exhibition Team dissolved, Welsh stayed on as an instructor for the Wright Company, at last fulfilling Wilbur and Orville's stated purpose for the Montgomery flight school to turn out flight instructors. In fact, he was the only one of the five students who remained in the Wright Company after the exhibition team dissolved. By some accounts he was the Wrights' best instructor. He certainly had the most lasting impact as an instructor in that he personally trained Hap Arnold, who one day would become a five-star general and the Air Chief of Staff for the Army in World War II.[332]

On June 11, 1912, Welsh was testing a new Wright airplane, recently purchased by the U.S. Army, at College Park, Maryland. Welsh, who was married and had an eight-year-old daughter, was a passenger while Army pilot Leighton Hazelhurst flew. Unfortunately, the airplane slammed into the ground after a seventy-five-foot dive. Both the pilot and Welsh were killed. Orville believed Hazelhurst had lost control of the craft, but further crashes of the newly designed "Model C" Wright airplane raised serious doubts about the Model C. After half of the Army's meager corps of twelve pilots had died in Model C crashes, a Wright instructor investigated the accidents and blamed poor maintenance. The Wright Company's own fac-tory manager, however, also investigated and concluded that the Model C's basic design was flawed. Promoting the factory manager to a research and development post, Orville was horrified when the man promptly grounded all Wright airplanes, Model C included, forcing a redesign.[333]

Brookins was the most famous and most successful of the Alabama students—and the only one of the three Montgomery graduate pilots to die

6860 A.S.

Above: *Arthur Welsh, far right, with some of his students. Leighton Hazelhurst is second from left. The two were killed in a crash a few days after this photo was taken.* Below: *Welsh, the best instructor among the Class of 1910's graduates, died June 11, 1912, in this crash at College Park, Maryland. Welsh was a passenger while he taught Hazelhurst, who also perished in the crash.*

in his bed rather than in a crash. After Brookins left Montgomery, he did briefly take on the role envisioned by the Wrights by training Frank Coffyn and Ralph Johnstone as pilots. Johnstone went on to become Hoxsey's in-house rival, entertaining crowds with a trumped-up battle between himself and Hoxsey at air shows. He died just as dramatically in a Denver air show a month and a half before Hoxsey—another casualty in a terrible run of ill luck for the Wright Company.[334]

Brookins survived his air show exploits, but not always easily. He recalled what happened when a competitor, Alfred Le Blanc, had a crash at a meet at Belmont in New York:

> He was on his last lap, flying low for greater speed. Something went wrong and he swooped down and hit a telephone pole. He hit it so hard that he took an eight-foot section out of the middle of the pole, leaving the upper part still suspended from the wires. The accident occurred at the far side of the field, so I decided to fly over and see what had happened.
>
> I took off into a 30-mile wind, rose to about 100 feet and then turned around and started with the wind. Just as I had straightened away, a connecting rod broke.
>
> Well, of course, the motor stopped, and there I was at a low altitude with a dead motor, and my own speed and the wind carrying me at 100 miles an hour. I tried to set her down as lightly as possible, but the light landing gear wouldn't stand the terrific speed. The first three or four somersaults were enough for me. I got off then, and what was left of the ship turned a dozen or so more. As for me, I had started out to see what had happened to Le Blanc. And when they brought him into the hospital tent, there I was lying on the operating table waiting for him.[335]

At an air show in Asbury Park, New Jersey, a few months after he left Montgomery, Brookins was besieged by press photographers and had to cut his motor on takeoff when they got in his way. He finally conjured up some space to take off. To his horror, when he was ready to land, there were fifty photographers right where he intended to touch down. He had already turned off his motor. "I did the only thing possible—nosed down from an elevation of fifty feet and tried to land in front of them," he explained later. "Well, all they had to do was raise the flap of the hospital tent and drag me in. I had a broken nose, a broken ankle and several teeth knocked out. And the ship was a complete wreck."[336]

Despite the wrecks, Brookins was a well-known stunt pilot. He also flew from Chicago to Springfield, Illinois, a whopping distance of 190 miles. Perhaps Wilbur had been right when he had ordered non-spectacular flights. The plain, ordinary, stunt-free flight to Springfield was heralded much as Orville had been heralded in Montgomery. Large crowds turned out in each town along Brookins's route, while trains blew their whistles and fire sirens screamed greetings. "The sky-gazers looked in astonishment as the great artificial bird bore down the heavens," the *Chicago Record Herald* reported. "Wonderment, surprise, absorption were written on every visage. [It was] a machine of travel that combined the speed of a locomotive with the comfort of the automobile, and in addition, sped through an element until now navigated only by the feathered kind. It was, in truth, the poetry of motion."[337]

The Montgomery venture had not turned out exactly as Wilbur and Orville had planned. Brookins did train some other pilots, including Hoxsey, but in the long run, he gained fame as a daredevil, not as the sober teacher the Wrights had hoped for. Welsh did become an instructor, but Crane and Davis did not, nor did Hoxsey. Thus, in that sense, the Alabama flight school did not achieve its grander plan of teaching the five students to become teachers of other pilots. The school did, on the other hand, launch three pilots and one airplane mechanic, with just one dropout. The pilots it turned out were certainly gutsy and often foolhardy, but they well knew how to fly. That fact itself turned out to be more urgently significant than expected. The insight the inventors of the airplane had amassed into controlling an aircraft might have died with them, had they not decided to open a pilot school. And Wilbur did die two years later of typhoid fever at age forty-five. As the inventor's father recorded sadly in his journal, "A short life, full of consequences."[338]

The Wrights had understood that they would someday have to turn over the controls to a new generation, and they had sought, in Alabama, to perfect the methodology of teaching. They were confident they had done so after that first class of pilots. In a brochure designed for the Wright Company School of Aviation near Dayton, which replaced the Montgomery school, the Wrights enumerated how training would unfold. Students would have a series of flights of five to fifteen minutes, totaling four actual hours in the air over at least eight days, if not more. There would be only four or five students per teacher, and every student would have individual instruction. "In all of the training flights the pupil is accompanied by the instructor . . .," the brochure advertised. "As the pupil begins to acquire the feel of the air, the instructor gradually relinquishes the levers to the pupil, but he is ever present and ready to resume control should the pupil make any serious mistake." The brochure commented that most students could master piloting after two to three hours of actual air time,[339] conveniently overlooking the many earthbound hours of balancing on the track, testing the winds, repairing broken parts, etc. The brochure described almost exactly the training course as it had unfolded in Montgomery. As the brochure boasted, "A course of training in this school is without question superior to any in this country, if not the world."[340] The Wrights had learned to fly at Kitty Hawk, but they had learned to teach flight in Alabama.

The city of Montgomery had had other goals for the flight school. In early 1910, Montgomery was looking to the future, with airplanes as a symbol of the "Young Man's Opportunity." By spring, the city had become the temporary aviation center of the world, its flying field swarming with tourists. For a brief moment in history, the city was, indeed, in the spotlight as it had so earnestly desired. If word did not get out about the area's great weather and kind hospitality, it was not because Montgomery didn't try. Even Orville Wright and his students ultimately cooperated in offering eye-catching, positive publicity about Montgomery. Thus, by one measure, Montgomery got what it wanted out of the Wright school. However, by the middle of 1910 the exciting world of aviation had bypassed the city.

As summer began in 1910, it appeared Montgomery would never be the home of a permanent flying center. Certainly students were no longer being taught there, and very few Montgomerians had actually gotten to take a flight. In that regard, many of Montgomery's dreams for the Wright school went unfulfilled. Over time, the Wright brothers' first civilian flying school, the historic night flights, and the day-to-day details of the camp were largely forgotten.

As part of the aviation class of 1910, the *Montgomery Advertiser* also learned its lessons. The Wrights had long been decried around the nation and world for their disinterest in good press relations. The celebrity inventors' refusal to court the press was grating in Montgomery, just as it grated everywhere else.[341] The media, as a whole, tended to make the underdog but press-friendly flyers such as Glenn Curtiss the heroes and the secretive Wrights the villains.[342] The *Montgomery Advertiser* staff was often irked about the Wright crew's smug secretiveness, causing negative coverage and unblushing snipes at the Wrights. However, as the *Advertiser* was surprised to discover, this negative press image played almost perfectly into the Wright brothers' plans to be left alone. If the famous brothers were unpopular with public and press, then just maybe some of the potential spectators would stay home. If the inventors of the airplane were painted as taciturn and unhelpful in the media, then visitors wouldn't be surprised when the Wright brothers and their crew were taciturn and unhelpful in the face of public curiosity.

In a dramatic lesson on how to have bad press relations and still come out as ultimate winners, Wilbur and Orville proved they were not only wizards in aviation, but also magicians in public relations. Their deliberately careless approach to their image worked. However, such laissez-faire public relations only work, as the Wrights showed, if you have just the right product. As their time in Montgomery proved, the inventors of the airplane had conquered a technology so awe-inspiring, so incredible, that even the most ill-natured detractor simply *had* to swallow his complaints and his disappointment and admit that the airplane was an amazing thing of beauty. Although the brothers wanted to cultivate the public's interest in flying machines, they did not have to do so by wooing the media. In the end, the media would come to woo them.

Thus, the Montgomery experience illustrated the fact that the Wright

*Spectacular flying such as this at Fort Myer, Virginia, in 1908 won praise for Orville in spite of the disastrous crash that killed Lieutenant Thomas Selfridge. Awed by the spectacle of flight, officials brushed off the fatality as unfortunate but insignificant.*

brothers didn't have to worry about their own public relations. The airplane itself was great enough without their cooperation. An extremely clear example of this happened prior to the Montgomery school when Orville crashed his airplane at Fort Myer, Virginia, on September 17, 1908, while attempting to meet flight standards set by the U.S. government. At the time the War Department was considering purchasing an airplane for military use. Orville's passenger, Lieutenant Thomas Selfridge, was killed in the crash, becoming the first person to die in a motorized airplane accident. The Washington, D.C., *Evening Star* ran an interview with Major George O. Squier, the top official dispatched by the government to assess the performance of the airplane. "We deplore the accident, but no one who saw the flights of the last four days at Fort Myer could doubt for an instant that the problem of aerial navigation was solved," the major said. "If Mr. Wright should never again enter an aeroplane his work last week at Ft. Myer will have secured him a lasting place in history as the man who showed the world that mechanical flight was an assured success."[343] With enthusiasm like that after a fatal crash, who needed to court good public relations? Wilbur and Orville could concentrate, as they wanted to, on their work, leaving their image to take care of itself—or, rather, to be taken care of by their invention.

As the nation's first flying school came to a close, one nagging question remained in tallying up the school's report card. Montgomery had sought great changes as the airplane landed at the Kohn plantation. Yet many Alabamians still clung to the humiliation of the Civil War as the defining point of Southern character. Despite the hopeful stars in Gilbert Edge's publicity cartoon, for many young men, the South was not the place of opportunity but of traditional, backbreaking labor in cotton and manufacturing and other hot, low-paying work. Of course, many others did find grand opportunity in Alabama. But after the Wrights left, much of the region was still poverty-stricken, uneducated, and divided by deep racial distrust.

Did the Wright brothers, then, inaugurate the new era of the South, as the *Advertiser* and much of Alabama had hoped they would? In one way they did, and oddly enough that way turned out to be via aviation. Blessed by a combination of war and tenacious leaders, the Kohn plantation survived as an air base. World War I thrust Montgomery back into the world of aviation, although on a much different scale than the celebrity-studded days of 1910. Montgomery at last had that Army post by World War I; in fact, the city could boast of *two* Army Air Service posts. One of them, Taylor Field, coincidentally was set up as a pilot training field that also handled airplane repairs. The old Kohn place was the second Army air post. Started in April 1918, the local name for the place was "Wright's Field," although officially it was Aviation Repair Depot #3. In a drastic change from the ad-covered "aerie," Aviation Repair Depot #3 featured fifty-two wooden buildings, including hangars, barracks, a post exchange, infirmary, and commissary. The post cost $819,000 to build. Governor Charles Henderson spoke at the opening ceremony for the new field in September 1918, noting that it was "the home of two pioneers in the aircraft game," the Wright brothers.[344]

After World War I, the depot nearly closed, but the War Department bought 302 acres outright from Frank Kohn in January 1920 for $34,137.92 with the intent, much pushed by post commander Major Louis R. Knight, to turn the depot into an aircraft manufacturing site—just as Montgomerians had hoped the Wrights would do back in 1910. The 1920 manufacturing plan didn't work out either, but in May 1922, the 4th Photo Section of the 22nd Observation Squadron arrived in Montgomery to take over the field. The flyers in the squadron carried out reconnaissance and photographic missions. Late in 1922, the post became known as Maxwell Field, named for a heroic Army Air Service pilot, Second Lieutenant William C. Maxwell, who died when he swerved his airplane on landing to avoid children in his way. Shortly Maxwell Field was slated to be closed again, but Congressman Lister Hill of Alabama managed to get federal funding for permanent buildings at Maxwell—the construction of which made it uneconomical for the Army to close the base. At last the old Wright flying field was a permanent air base.[345]

Orville Wright visited his former pilot school grounds in 1945 when a training facility for pilots of heavy bombers was dedicated at Maxwell. Today, still in keeping with the Wright tradition of pilot training, the former Kohn plantation is now home to Maxwell's Air University and a host of other high-level air education schools. When Air University was started in 1946, Maxwell was already home to Air Tactical School for junior officers, Air Command and Staff School for middle-rank officers, and Air War College for high-ranking personnel. Air University itself was envisioned as a graduate school for career Air Force officers to prepare for the future of war in the air. Later the base opened another school for educating flyers—the postgraduate School for Advanced Air Power Studies.[346] The high involvement of Montgomery with air education would seem to be more a coincidence than a direct relationship to the Wright pilot school—but then again, it seems the former Kohn plantation has some sort of ongoing magnetism for air educators.

The existence of Maxwell Air Force Base and Air University and the other Air Force schools in Montgomery can be traced at least tangentially to the Wright presence. Major Walter R. Weaver, Maxwell post commander

*Orville Wright as he appeared around the time he visited Maxwell Field, the site of his old Alabama flying school, in 1945.*

in 1929, always thought that the location of the base had been determined during World War I "largely because of its early history under the Wright Brothers."[347] And certainly the receptivity of people to airplanes brought more local support and more interest as Maxwell developed in the World War I era—perhaps more than might have been found in various other cities that had never been graced by an airplane.

The next great war brought Alabama another important connection to the teaching of flight. Not far from Montgomery, at Tuskegee Institute, a project to train black pilots took shape. The Tuskegee Airmen proved to a doubting military that black pilots could fly and that men of color could succeed in the armed services. After World War II, Alabama would take another giant leap forward in flight by becoming home to German rocket scientist Wernher von Braun and his entourage of scientists, who worked out of Huntsville to help launch America's space program.

It is doubtful that there was much direct connection between either the Tuskegee Airmen or von Braun's rocket program and the Wright brothers, the Wrights having been all but forgotten as Alabama aviation heroes by then. However, in a state stigmatized worldwide for backward thinking, the major flight breakthroughs in Alabama belied old prejudices. The supposedly backward-looking Alabamians were as forward-looking as Montgomery's Commercial Club after all, when it came to flight. As the club had realized, the flying machine was the high road away from the beaten-down past of the Confederacy. Airplanes were separate and distinct from Confederate history, and thus powered flight could help create a Southern future without causing any misgivings about honoring or dishonoring the past. Aviation brought with it no record of regional failure and humiliation to claim as part of the Southern identity.

As Alabama became an aviation center throughout the twentieth century, it seemed that aviation itself was, indeed, a key player in the future, as the Commercial Club had hoped it would be in 1910. Southerners in general and Alabamians in particular understood flight as a step toward a glorious time ahead, away from the bad times of the past. As Gilbert Edge had seen it, so other Alabamians saw it across time: Alabama offered "The Young Man's Opportunity"—especially if an aircraft danced tantalizingly above all.

◡

*This monument at Maxwell Air Force Base was placed on the site of the long-gone Wright flying school hangar, in honor of Montgomery's first great leap into the sky.*

# Notes

## Introduction—The Yearbook That Never Was

1   Wilbur Wright to Octave Chanute, May 13, 1900, reprinted in Phil Scott, ed., *The Pioneers of Flight: A Documentary History* (Princeton, N.J.: Princeton University Press, 1999), p. 86.

2   Orville Wright, "How We Invented the Airplane," and Orville Wright, "After the First Flights," pp. 11–21 and pp. 45–46, respectively, in Orville Wright, *How We Invented the Airplane: An Illustrated History*, ed. Fred C. Kelly (New York: Dover, 1953, with new text added in 1988. The work encompasses writings by Orville Wright circa 1920. Page numbers refer to 1988 edition.).

3   Sherwood Harris, *First to Fly: Aviation's Pioneer Days* (Blue Ridge Summit, Pa.: Tab/Aero Books), p. 112.

4   See Harris, pp. 114, 116 on training of pilots. As to the reluctance of the government to acquire an airplane, a remarkable series of letters between the U.S. government and the Wright brothers survives. The government simply couldn't fathom that the Wrights had perfected flight and kept turning down their offer to sell the military a flyer. Instead, the various government officials the Wrights contacted all seemed to gloss over the Wrights' claims of flight and assumed they wanted cash to *develop* a flying machine. See Wilbur and Orville Wright to Congressman Robert M. Nevin, January 18, 1905; Major General G. L. Gillespie to Congressman Nevin, undated; Wilbur and Orville Wright to Secretary of War William H. Taft, October 9, 1905; Major General J. C. Bates to Wilbur and Orville Wright, October 16, 1905; Wilbur and Orville Wright to the President of the Board of Ordnance and Fortification, War Department, October 19, 1906; Minutes, Board of Ordnance and Fortification, October 24, 1905; and Orville Wright to Board of Ordnance and Fortification, War Department, May 17, 1907, all reprinted in Scott, pp. 137–140.

5   Fred C. Kelly, "After Kitty Hawk: A Brief Résumé," in Orville Wright, *How We Invented the Airplane,* pp. 51–52.

6   More detailed information on these factors of the Wright school will be documented as the story unfolds.

7   On Knabenshue, see Fred Howard, *Wilbur and Orville: A Biography of the Wright Brothers* (New York: Alfred A. Knopf, 1987), p. 353; see also Richard P. Hallion, ed., *The Wright Brothers: Heirs of Prometheus* (Washington, D.C.: Smithsonian Institution Press, 1978), p. 134 in "A Chronology of The Wright Brothers, 1867–1948."

8   "Two Ohio Brothers Crowned With Success," *Norfolk Virginian-Pilot,* December 18, 1903, reprinted in Scott, p. 128.

9   Orville Wright, diary, December 17, 1903, reprinted in Scott, p. 124.

10   "Airship that Flew in North Carolina and its Inventors," drawing accompanying Associated Press, "Flying Machine Problem Solved by Ohio Man," *Milwaukee Daily News* (Wisconsin), December 18, 1903, p. 1.

11   Wright brothers, statement to the Associated Press, January 5, 1904, reprinted in Scott, p. 132.

12   Wilbur and Orville published, all in Dayton, Ohio, the *West Side News, The Evening Item,* the *Dayton Tattler,* and *Snap Shots at Current Events.* Orville was just 17 when the *West Side News* was first issued, and Wilbur was 22. The *Tattler* was oriented toward

Dayton's black readers. The brothers gave up the printing business for bicycle building, and that job gave way to inventing and producing the airplane. See Charlotte K. and August E. Brunsman, *Wright & Wright, Printers: The Other Career of Wilbur and Orville* (1988 booklet; available at Dayton [Ohio] Aviation Heritage National Historic Park).

13  Wilbur Wright to Octave Chanute, January 20, 1910, and Octave Chanute to Wilbur Wright, January 23, 1910, reprinted in Scott, pp. 176–177.

14  "The Wright Brothers' Aeroplane in France and the United States," *Scientific American* XCIX (August 29, 1908), p. 141.

15  "Wilbur Wright Jokes Brother," *Montgomery Advertiser* (Alabama), March 31, 1910, p. 5.

## Chapter 1—The Runway to the Future, 1910

16  For example, a handsome photo of General Clement A. Evans, a Confederate veteran in full military regalia, appeared on the front page of the *Montgomery Advertiser*, April 26, 1910, p. 1.

17  United States Army, Air Corps Tactical School (Maxwell Field, Ala.), *Maxwell Field: Army Air Corps* (Montgomery, Ala.: Air Corps Tactical School, 1929), p. 48.

18  Gilbert Edge, "Howdy!" (cartoon), *Montgomery Advertiser*, May 11, 1910, p. 4. See also *Minutes of the Fourteenth Annual Convention, Alabama Division, Daughters of the Confederacy* (Opelika, Ala.: Post Publishing, 1910), whose cover gives Montgomery as the convention locale.

19  "Orville Wright Repairs Engine," *Montgomery Advertiser*, April 7, 1910, p. 5. The "White House of the Confederacy," now located across the street from the Capitol building, was at the time several blocks away.

20  Wayne Flynt, *Montgomery: An Illustrated History* (Woodland Hills, Calif.: Windsor Publications, 1980), p. 60. The claim that Montgomery's trolley system was first in the world comes up occasionally, although most settle for the title of first in the nation. One source that claims first in the world is U.S. Army, *Maxwell Field: Army Air Corps*, p. 49. That in-house history of Maxwell spells the trolley designer's last name as "Vanderpoel" and supplies the additional information that the Belgian lived in Detroit. As the sources note, the first trial run of the streetcar came in 1885, with the complete system in place in 1886.

21  Roger Alston Jones, "Montgomery, Our Opportunity," speech reprinted in *Montgomery Advertiser*, May 1, 1910, p. 8.

22  Ibid.

23  Ibid.

24  Ibid.

25  Associated Press, "Air Ships for Carnival," *Montgomery Advertiser*, January 31, 1910, p. 3. The *Montgomery Advertiser* never spelled out the Associated Press as the author of articles that were not locally written; however, the newspaper did advertise that it used Associated Press material. All stories with a dateline before the lead of the article have been deemed written by the Associated Press, following the datelined Associated Press format of today.

26  "Misrepresent State Schools," *Montgomery Advertiser*, January 5, 1910, p. 3, based on an article by Alice C. Biddle in the *Journal of Education*.

27  Gordon McKinley, "The Fine Sheep Ranch on the Hunter Vaughan Place," *Montgomery Advertiser*, January 11, 1910, p. 14.

28  Gordon McKinley, "Japanese Kudzu Vine and Cassava as Food For Stock," *Montgomery*

*Advertiser*, January 12, 1910, p. 5.

29   "Mayor Planning Wider Streets," *Montgomery Advertiser*, January 11, 1910, p. 7.

30   Alfred J. Stofer, "Alabama Will Get Good Sum," *Montgomery Advertiser,* January 12, 1910, p. 9.

31   "Montgomery May Get Post," *Montgomery Advertiser*, January 18, 1910, p. 7.

32   "South Getting the Benefits of Publicity Campaign," *Montgomery Advertiser*, February 1, 1910, p. 4.

33   Ibid.

34   Associated Press, "Ready for Airships," *Montgomery Advertiser*, January 9, 1910, p. 31.

35   Associated Press, "America Takes Flying Honors," *Montgomery Advertiser*, January 12, 1910, p. 12.

36   Associated Press, "Paulhan Sets Height Record," *Montgomery Advertiser*, January 13, 1910, p. 10.

37   Associated Press, "Paulhan Defies Gravity's Laws," *Montgomery Advertiser*, January 19, 1910, p. 1.

38   Gilbert Edge, "It Shines for All" (cartoon), *Montgomery Advertiser,* February 2, 1910, p. 4.

39   Orville Wright to Glenn Curtiss, July 20, 1908, reprinted in Scott, p. 161.

40   Special of the *Chicago* (Illinois) *Times-Herald*, distributed to other newspapers and reprinted as "Flying Craft Made Perfect" in *The Weekly News* (Denver, Colo.), July 13, 1899, p. 4.

41   Stephen Kirk, *First in Flight: The Wright Brothers in North Carolina* (Winston-Salem, N.C.: John F. Blair, 1995), pp. 174–175.

42   *Chicago Times-Herald*, reprinted as "Flying Craft Made Perfect," *Weekly News*, July 13, 1899, p. 4. The Great Aerodrome has since been deemed unflyable. Kirk, p. 167, notes it was very flimsily built in an attempt to make it light. Charles Gibbs-Smith, *Early Flying Machines, 1799–1909* (London: Eyre Methuen, 1975), cites structural flaws and adds that the Aerodrome was not able to fly due to aerodynamic flaws. Gibbs-Smith also offers a dramatic photo of the Aerodrome falling into the Potomac. See pp. 51–52.

43   Curtis Prendergast, *The First Aviators* (Alexandria, Va.: Time-Life, 1980). See "The Wrights vs. the World," Chapter 4, pp. 115–135, for an in-depth discussion of Wright patent problems and effects of the patents on early aviation. Prendergast also discusses distrust of the Wrights, due to their secrecy, throughout the book. See, for instance, pp. 19–20, 29, 31–35. Howard deals with the patent issue throughout *Wilbur and Orville*, but see particularly Chapter 42, "Who Invented Wingwarping?" pp. 362–370. See also Kirk, pp. 269–276, 280–292.

44   "The Wright Aeroplane Test in North Carolina," *Scientific American* XCVIII (May 30, 1908): 393.

45   Ibid.

46   "First Flights of the Aerial Experiment Association's Second Aeroplane," *Scientific American* XCVIII (May 30, 1908): 392.

47   Orville Wright to Glenn Curtiss, July 20, 1908, reprinted in Scott, p. 161.

48   "Wright Brothers Will Soon Be In Montgomery To Begin Flying School," *Birmingham Age-Herald* (Alabama), March 24, 1910, p. 1. The *Age-Herald*'s aviation reports were often labeled as being "special," i.e., written by a special correspondent. On one occasion, the *Age-Herald* named its special correspondent as Hervey W. Laird. It is possible that Laird wrote all of the *Age-Herald*'s Wright stories, although some originated from distant places such as New York and Laird probably did not write them. As with other

journalistic sources, no author designation will be given for *Age-Herald* stories that did not name a specific reporter.

49   Associated Press, "License Meet as a Whole," *Montgomery Advertiser*, April 28, 1910, p. 10. The first air show to be licensed as a whole was the one the Wright student pilots from Montgomery flew in at Indianapolis, Indiana, shortly after they left Montgomery. The air show took place in June 1910, although the licensing process was worked out in April of that year.

50   Associated Press, "Curtis Won't Contest," *Montgomery Advertiser*, January 21, 1910, p. 4.

51   Associated Press, "Air Ships for Carnival," *Montgomery Advertiser*, January 31, 1910, p. 3.

52   "Wizard of Air to Locate Here," *Montgomery Advertiser*, February 16, 1910, p. 7.

53   "The Wright Brothers' Aeroplane in France And The United States," *Scientific American* XCLX (August 29, 1908): 140–141.

54   "Alabama to Washington Via Air Line is Birmingham Inventor's Plan," *Montgomery Advertiser*, February 14, 1910, p. 2.

55   Ibid.

56   Ibid.

57   See, for example, Associated Press, "Paulhan Wins $50,000 Prize," *Montgomery Advertiser*, April 28, 1910, p. 1, which saw Louis Paulhan win a large cash prize for a flight of 186 miles—with a stop partway there.

58   "Alabama to Washington Via Air Line," *Montgomery Advertiser*, February 14, 1910, p. 2.

59   "E. T. Odum's flying machine is displayed at the 1909 Alabama State Fair," Southern Museum of Flight (Birmingham, Ala.) photo, reprinted in Don Dodd and Amy Bartlett Dodd, *Deep South Aviation* (Charleston, S.C.: Arcadia, 1999), p. 14.

60   "Odom Makes Aeroplane Trials," *Birmingham Age-Herald*, March 30, 1910, p. 4; also, "E. T. Odum's flying machine," pictured in Dodd and Dodd, p. 14. Odum's name appears as "Odom" in some sources.

61   "An early 'Flying Machine' built by John Fowler," pictured in Dodd and Dodd, p. 6.

62   Dr. Boswell's plantation is now part of the Talladega Superspeedway in Talladega, Alabama. The Talladega Motor Sports Museum has an exhibit dedicated to his claim of having beaten the Wrights. The exhibit cites Landon C. Bell, PhD, "Dr. Boswell Invents An Aeroplane," *The Old Free State*, volume 2.

63   Gilbert Edge, "Up in the Air" (cartoon), *Montgomery Advertiser*, January 30, 1910, p. 4.

64   Gilbert Edge, "Soaring" (cartoon), *Montgomery Advertiser*, January 14, 1910, p. 4. Complaints about high food costs of the era abounded in the *Montgomery Advertiser*. As an example, see Montgomery Fair Department Store's advertisement that it provided "Wholesome Groceries Rightly Priced" and took only a small profit, as well as Edge's cartoon "Contrast" in the *Montgomery Advertiser* of February 13, 1910, p. 4.

65   W. Stewart Duncan, "Maybe the Martians are Like Big Insects," *Montgomery Advertiser*, March 6, 1910, p. 20.

## Chapter 2—The School Is Founded

66   "Wizard of Air to Locate Here," *Montgomery Advertiser*, February 16, 1910, p. 7.

67   Fred S. Ball, "The Genesis of Maxwell Field at Montgomery, Alabama," pp. 7–13, in U.S. Army, *Maxwell Field: Army Air Corps*, p. 7. The description of Ball as dapper is based on a photo of him in Jerome A. Ennels and Wesley Phillips Newton, *The Wisdom*

*of Eagles: A History of Maxwell Air Force Base* (Montgomery, Ala.: Black Belt Press, 1997), p. 14. Ball's age is derived from Thomas McAdory Owen, *History of Alabama and Dictionary of Alabama Biography* III (Chicago: S. J. Clarke, 1921), p. 84.

68  Wilbur Wright, diary, quoted in Harris, p. 116.

69  Ball, in U.S. Army, *Maxwell Field: Army Air Corps*, p. 7.

70  "Wizard of Air to Locate Here," *Montgomery Advertiser*, February 16, 1910, p. 7.

71  Ibid.

72  Ibid. None of the *Montgomery Advertiser*'s reports on the Wright brothers were signed. The writing style seems consistent throughout the vast majority of the Wright articles, indicating that likely the same reporter had the "aeroplane beat." This has been assumed throughout the book. The few articles that were inconsistent in writing style were extremely short ones, which gave out brief facts.

73  "Wrights Order 'Aerie' Built," *Montgomery Advertiser*, March 2, 1910, p. 7. By March 2 when this article was written, Ball could credit the telegram campaign of February with successfully wooing the Wrights. The content of the telegrams was not spelled out in the article, but the *Montgomery Advertiser* implied they promised aid.

74  "Wizard of Air to Locate Here," *Montgomery Advertiser*, February 16, 1910, p. 7. For a comparison to the retail cost of the airplane, note the $7,500 price tag of a Wright flyer in "Wright Forces Here For Work," *Montgomery Advertiser*, March 21, 1910, p. 5.

75  "Wizard of Air to Locate Here," *Montgomery Advertiser*, February 16, 1910, p. 7.

76  Ibid.

77  Ibid.

78  Ibid.

79  "Selects Site for an 'Aerie,'" *Montgomery Advertiser*, February 17, 1910, p. 10. The *Montgomery Advertiser* did not specify the crop grown on the plantation, but Ennels and Newton say it was cotton. See Ennels and Newton, pp. 13–14. Ball, in U.S. Army, *Maxwell Field: Army Air Corps*, recalled things differently than they were portrayed in the *Montgomery Advertiser*. Some two decades after the Wright school, Ball wrote that he personally had asked Kohn to consider giving up his land for the flying field on the day Wilbur arrived. See p. 7. However, the *Montgomery Advertiser* reported that the matter was settled over a couple of days' time. Given the fact that the newspaper managed to fill space on Wilbur's search for more than one day and given the fact that Ball was recalling events years later, it is likely that the *Montgomery Advertiser*'s account is the more accurate. For Kohn's profession, see an advertisement he placed, "F. M. Kohn & Son, Real Estate and Insurance," *Montgomery Advertiser*, January 30, 1910, p. 26.

80  Society of Pioneers of Montgomery, *100 Years, 100 Families* (Montgomery, Ala.: Society of Pioneers of Montgomery, 1958), p. 35; see also Kohn's picture in Ennels and Newton, p. 14.

81  "Selects Site for an 'Aerie,'" *Montgomery Advertiser*, February 17, 1910, p. 10.

82  "Wrights on Way to Montgomery," *Birmingham Age-Herald*, March 18, 1910, p. 3.

83  "Selects Site for an 'Aerie,'" *Montgomery Advertiser*, February 17, 1910, p. 10.

84  Ibid.

85  Ibid.

86  Ibid.

87  Ibid.

88  Ibid.

89  "Flyers' Coming Boosts Capital," *Montgomery Advertiser*, February 18, 1910, p. 3.

90  Ibid. That John and Frank Kohn were brothers is confirmed by the U.S. Census.

91 Ibid.

92 Ball, in U.S. Army, *Maxwell Field: Army Air Corps,* p. 7.

93 "Flyers' Coming Boosts Capital," *Montgomery Advertiser,* February 18, 1910, p. 3.

94 Ibid.

95 Owens, IV, p. 1516.

96 Associated Press, "For Aeroplane Factory Here," *Montgomery Advertiser,* February 20, 1910, p. 28.

97 Ibid.

98 Gilbert Edge, "With Wright" (cartoon), *Montgomery Advertiser,* February 24, 1910, p. 4. The cartoonist mistakenly missed the "s" in "us."

99 "Wrights Order 'Aerie' Built," *Montgomery Advertiser,* March 2, 1910, p. 7.

100 "Selects Site for an 'Aerie,'" *Montgomery Advertiser,* February 17, 1910, p. 10. The article spelled the city name of Pau, France, phonetically as "Poe."

101 "Wrights Order 'Aerie' Built," *Montgomery Advertiser,* March 2, 1910, p. 7.

102 Ibid. The writer said Wilbur had left three weeks earlier, but that was incorrect. He had arrived a little more than two weeks earlier and had left shortly thereafter.

103 "Aeroplane in Capital," *Montgomery Advertiser,* March 16, 1910, p. 9. As to the description of the station, see Montgomery Museum of Fine Arts, *Spaces and Places: Views of Montgomery's Built Environment* (Montgomery, Ala: Montgomery Museum of Fine Arts, 1978), p. 39.

104 "Wrights Order 'Aerie' Built," *Montgomery Advertiser,* March 2, 1910, p. 7.

105 "Wright's Bird Takes to Air," *Montgomery Advertiser,* March 27, 1910, p. 16.

106 "Wrights Order 'Aerie' Built," *Montgomery Advertiser,* March 2, 1910, p. 7.

107 Ibid.

108 Business Men's League of Montgomery, *Montgomery, Alabama* (New York: Moses King, 1910) (booklet with unnumbered pages), photos and cutlines of Bell Building and First National Bank Building. The reference to their heights, later in the paragraph, comes from this source as well. See also *The Heritage of Montgomery County, Alabama* (Clanton, Ala.: Heritage Publishing Consultants, 2001), p. 28. Also see Montgomery Museum of Fine Arts, p. 15.

109 "Wrights Order 'Aerie' Built," *Montgomery Advertiser,* March 2, 1910, p. 7.

110 "Wrights Will Soon be in Air," *Montgomery Advertiser,* March 9, 1910, p. 11.

111 "Prepare for Aeronaut," *Montgomery Advertiser,* March 7, 1910, p. 6.

112 Associated Press, "Wright Brothers Will Soon Be in Montgomery to Begin Flying School," *Birmingham Age-Herald,* March 24, 1910, p. 1. The article was produced by a wire service, as it featured a dateline from Washington, where the Wrights were receiving a medal. Since some information later in the article was duplicated in Associated Press, "Wrights Start for Dixie Camp," *Montgomery Advertiser,* March 23, 1910, p. 9, it seems the *Age-Herald* article was also by Associated Press. Regarding the number of pilots in the United States, see Harris, pp. 114, 116.

113 "Wizard of Air to Locate Here," *Montgomery Advertiser,* February 16, 1910, p. 7.

114 "Wrights Soon Will be in Air," *Montgomery Advertiser,* March 9, 1910, p. 11.

115 Unsigned editorial, "The Wright Brothers Opportunity," *Montgomery Advertiser,* March 9, 1910, p. 4. The editorials in the *Montgomery Advertiser* were never signed, but W. W. Screws was listed as the president of the Advertiser Company. Although Screws was not the only *Montgomery Advertiser* staff member mentioned in the masthead, the implication was that Screws handled editorials. Besides Screws, whose name and title were given at the very top of the editorial box, there was F. P. Glass, who was also listed

at the top of the editorial box. However, he was listed as secretary-treasurer. According to Owen, Glass controlled the business side, leaving Screws to control the editorial side of the newspaper. See Owen, IV, p. 1516. Lower down on the list, the masthead named a circulation manager, a publisher's representative, and an advertising manager. Conspicuously absent from the masthead in 1910 was William Thomas Sheehan, who had become assistant editor to Screws in 1907. See Owen, IV, p. 1539. Owen clearly considered Screws to be the editorial writer, instead of Sheehan. Indeed, Sheehan was involved in a public relations stunt for the newspaper in early June, 1910, perhaps indicating he had more of a PR role at the newspaper at that time. He and cartoonist Gilbert Edge, along with Ben Screws, walked to Troy, Brundidge, and Ozark, Alabama, and their journey was covered by the *Montgomery Advertiser*. See "Ben Screws Turns Ankle," *Montgomery Advertiser*, June 4, 1910, p. 8. This book will assume that W. W. Screws, not Sheehan, wrote the editorials during the Wright brothers' era in Montgomery. In any case, as the president listed in the masthead, Screws would have been given official credit (or blame) for the editorials, no matter who penned them.

116 Unsigned editorial, "The Wright Brothers Opportunity," *Montgomery Advertiser*, March 9, 1910, p. 4.

117 "Wrights Soon Will be in Air," *Montgomery Advertiser*, March 9, 1910, p. 11.

118 "Wrights Will Ship Machine," *Montgomery Advertiser*, March 10, 1910, p. 10.

119 Ball, in U.S. Army, *Maxwell Field: Army Air Corps*, p. 11.

120 "Wrights Will Ship Machine," *Montgomery Advertiser*, March 10, 1910, p. 10.

121 "Wrights Soon Will be in Air," *Montgomery Advertiser*, March 9, 1910, p. 11.

122 "Wrights Will Ship Machine," *Montgomery Advertiser*, March 10, 1910, p. 10.

123 Ibid.

124 "Await Wrights' Coming," *Montgomery Advertiser*, March 13, 1910, p. 13.

125 "Eyes Turn on Wright Camp," *Montgomery Advertiser*, March 18, 1910, p. 12.

126 "Aeroplane in Capital," *Montgomery Advertiser*, March 16, 1910, p. 9.

127 "Eyes Turn on Wright Camp," *Montgomery Advertiser*, March 18, 1910, p. 12.

128 Ibid.

129 Ibid.

130 Photograph number 69 in Orville Wright, *How We Invented the Airplane*, Kelly's edited 1953 edition. The photo is on p. 75. Also, there is a photo of the structure on page 17, Ennels and Newton. To see the roof advertisement, see U.S. Army, *Maxwell Field: Army Air Corps*, p. 9. The message about St. Regis Coffee was pieced together based on photos in Orville Wright, p. 75, and Flynt, p. 73, as well as Society of Pioneers of Montgomery, *A History of Montgomery in Pictures* (Montgomery, Ala.: Society of Pioneers of Montgomery, 1963), p. 36. Apparently when the hangar doors were shut, the two doors (which stood open while the Wright crew was there) came together to make the message about the coffee.

131 "Eyes Turn on Wright Camp," *Montgomery Advertiser*, March 18, 1910, p. 12; see also picture, Ennels and Newton, p. 17.

132 Business Men's League of Montgomery, panoramic photo of downtown in 1910, un-numbered page; see also *City Directory and History of Montgomery, Alabama* (Montgomery, Ala: T. C. Brigham, 1878), advertisement on endpapers; also see Wayne Greenhaw, *Montgomery: The River City* (Montgomery, Ala.: River City Publishing, 2002), p. 120. Mary Ann Neeley, *Montgomery: Capital City Corners* (Dover, N.H.: Arcadia, 1997), p. 41, reprints an 1898 playbill for Montgomery Theater advertising The Fair. Tom Connor, *Remember When* (*Montgomery Montgomery Advertiser and Alabama Journal*, 1989) gives the date of Pollaks' founding (unnumbered page; 164th vignette. Reprinted from

the *Montgomery Advertiser*, original date of publication in the newspaper not given). For items carried by Montgomery Fair in 1910, see ads by the store in the *Montgomery Advertiser*, March 20, 1910, p. 28, and March 25, 1910, p. 9.

133 Montgomery Fair, "Sale of Air Ships" (advertisement), *Montgomery Advertiser,* March 20, 1910, p. 28.

134 Southern Shoe Surgery, "Wright Bros. Given Cordial Invitation" (advertisement), *Montgomery Advertiser,* April 10, 1910, p. 28.

135 "Turns Liberty's Head," *New York Tribune* (New York City), September 20, 1909, p. 1.

136 "Begin to Build Flying Machine," *Montgomery Advertiser,* March 20, 1910, p. 11.

137 Ibid.

138 Ball, in U.S. Army, *Maxwell Field: Army Air Corps*, p. 8. The unnamed editor of *Maxwell Field* made a point of saying that Orville approved Ball's manuscript for accuracy. Barring any memory loss by Orville, the airplane's description by Ball was therefore accurate.

## Chapter 3—The Great Spectator Sport

139 "Begin to Build Flying Machine," *Montgomery Advertiser,* March 20, 1910, p. 11.

140 "Wright Forces Here For Work," *Montgomery Advertiser,* March 21, 1910, p. 5.

141 Charles E. Taylor, "My Story," as told to Robert S. Ball, in *Air Line Pilot* (April 2000), reprint of a 1948 article from *Collier's* (December 25, 1948); available at http://www.centennialofflight.gov/wbh/charlestaylor.htm.

142 "Wright Forces Here For Work," *Montgomery Advertiser,* March 21, 1910, p. 5.

143 Ibid.

144 "Great Mechanical Bird of Wright Brothers Begins to Assume Definite Shape Under Deft Hands of Workmen at Training Camp," *Montgomery Advertiser,* March 22, 1910, p. 7.

145 Ibid.

146 Ibid.

147 Ibid.

148 "Wizards of Air Plan for Flights in Montgomery," *Montgomery Advertiser*, March 23, 1910, p. 9.

149 Associated Press, "Wrights Start for Dixie Camp," *Montgomery Advertiser*, March 23, 1910, p. 9.

150 Dr. [Richard] Stimson, "Wright Company Flying School," subsection of "The World's First Flying Field," available at http://www.wrightstories.com, located in the site's archives, subsection "Wright Activities After 1903." Stimson's article quoted a brochure produced for the flying school at Simms Station outside of Dayton, Ohio, which had the formal name of the Wright Company School of Aviation. That school immediately followed the Montgomery school. It is likely that the tuition was the same in Montgomery. The brochure noted that the Simms Station school was "a permanent school of aviation," an apparent attempt to eliminate confusion over the Montgomery school, which had turned out not to be permanent.

151 "Wizard of Air Here for Work," *Montgomery Advertiser*, March 25, 1910, p. 10.

152 Montgomery Museum of Fine Arts, p. 11 (from an introduction by Milo Howard), and Neeley, p. 18. Also see Society of Pioneers of Montgomery, *A History . . .*, photo of historic plaque, p. 40; also, Business Men's League of Montgomery, photo and caption of the later Exchange, unnumbered page.

153 "Wizard of Air Here for Work," *Montgomery Advertiser*, March 25, 1910, p. 10.

154 Ball, in U.S. Army, *Maxwell Field: Army Air Corps*, pp. 12–13.

155 "Wizard of Air Here for Work," *Montgomery Advertiser*, March 25, 1910, p. 10. The "Brookie" nickname was given by Tom D. Crouch, *The Bishop's Boys: A Life of Wilbur and Orville Wright* (New York: W. W. Norton, 1989), p. 426.

156 Crouch, p. 462; see also Howard, p. 353. Also see The Frank Coffyn Collection, "The Collection: People: Walter Brookins," available at http://www.centennialofflight.gov/coffyn/php, and "Brookins Flies Baby Grand," available at http://www.earlyaviators.com/ebrookin, in "Walter R. Brookins, 1889–1953." As to the Frank Coffyn collection, Coffyn was an early Wright pilot who knew Brookins and the other Wright students of the 1910 school; the material comes from his scrapbook.

157 "1908, Fort Myer, Virginia," photo and cutline, available at http://www.centennialofflight.gov/wbh.

158 "Wright's Bird Takes to Air," *Montgomery Advertiser*, March 21, 1910, p. 16.

159 "Orville Wright Plans Changes," *Montgomery Advertiser*, March 26, 1910, p. 3.

160 Unsigned, untitled editorial, *Montgomery Advertiser*, March 26, 1910, p. 4.

161 "Wright's Bird Takes to Air," *Montgomery Advertiser*, March 27, 1910, p. 16.

162 Ibid.

163 Ennels and Newton, p. 13.

164 "Orville Wright is Busy," *Birmingham Age-Herald*, March 26, 1910, p. 3.

165 Hervey W. Laird, "Orville Wright Makes his Initial Flight in Alabama," *Birmingham Age-Herald*, March 27, 1910, p. 3.

166 Ibid.

167 Ibid.

168 Ennels and Newton, p. 15.

169 Laird, "Orville Wright Makes his Initial Flight in Alabama," *Birmingham Age-Herald*, March 27, 1910, p. 3.

170 Ibid.

171 "Orville Wright Flies for Miles," *Montgomery Advertiser*, March 29, 1910, p. 12.

172 Ibid.

173 Ibid.

174 Laird, "Orville Wright Makes his Initial Flight in Alabama," *Birmingham Age-Herald*, March 27, 1910, p. 3.

175 "Big Aeroplane Lies Dormant," *Montgomery Advertiser*, March 30, 1910, p. 3. The bracketed word in the quote originally read "is," following what was apparently proper grammar usage in its day. That grammatical construction—a singular where today we would put a plural—cropped up frequently.

176 "Big Aeroplane Lies Dormant," *Montgomery Advertiser*, March 30, 1910, p. 3.

177 "Wilbur Wright Jokes Brother," *Montgomery Advertiser*, March 31, 1910, p. 5.

178 Ibid.

179 Associated Press, "Flyer Hurled to Awful Death," *Montgomery Advertiser*, April 3, 1910, p. 1.

180 Associated Press, "Wounded Men Drop Almost From Clouds to Death in Sea," *Montgomery Advertiser*, April 4, 1910, p. 1.

181 Associated Press, "German Aeronaut Killed," *Montgomery Advertiser*, April 5, 1910, p. 1.

182 Unsigned editorial, "One More Example," *Montgomery Advertiser*, April 6, 1910, p. 4.

183 Unsigned editorial, "Hot Air Talk," *Montgomery Advertiser*, April 11, 1910, p. 4.

184 Unsigned editorial, "A Nation of Doubters," *Montgomery Advertiser,* April 18, 1910, p. 4.

185 Unsigned editorial, "Montgomery's Good Fortune," *Birmingham Age-Herald,* April 1910, p. 36.

## Chapter 4—The Professor at Work

186 "Wright Buffets Gusty Breezes," *Montgomery Advertiser,* April 2, 1910, p. 10.

187 Orville Wright, "Possibilities of Soaring Flight," pp. 157–161 in Peter L. Jakab and Rick Young, eds., *The Published Writings of Wilbur and Orville Wright* (Washington, D.C.: Smithsonian Institution Press, 2000), p. 160. Orville had originally published the piece in *U.S. Air Service,* December 1922, pp. 7–9.

188 "Vacation for Aviators," *Montgomery Advertiser,* April 10, 1910, p. 13.

189 "Will Not Enter Field of Auto," *Montgomery Advertiser,* April 5, 1910, p. 12.

190 "Wright Adds to List of Pupils," *Montgomery Advertiser,* April 6, 1910, p. 8.

191 Ibid. See also Frank Coffyn Collection, "The Collection: People: Archibald Hoxsey."

192 Howard, p. 353, and Crouch, p. 427. See also Frank Coffyn Collection, "The Collection: People: Roy Knabenshue."

193 "Orville Wright Repairs Engine," *Montgomery Advertiser,* April 7, 1910, p. 5.

194 Ibid.

195 Ibid.

196 "Women Eager for Flight," *Montgomery Advertiser,* April 8, 1910, p. 9.

197 Ibid.

198 Associated Press, "Curtiss Breaks World's Record," *Montgomery Advertiser,* April 8, 1910, p. 9.

199 "Women Eager for Flight," *Montgomery Advertiser,* April 8, 1910, p. 9.

200 Ibid.

201 Associated Press, "France Also Has a Flying School," *Montgomery Advertiser,* April 10, 1910, p. 7.

202 "Wright Goes to Dayton," *Montgomery Advertiser,* April 9, 1910, p. 5.

203 "Vacation for Aviators," *Montgomery Advertiser,* April 10, 1910, p. 13.

204 Associated Press, "Aviator Falls on Automobile," *Montgomery Advertiser,* April 11, 1910, p. 1.

205 Frank Coffyn Collection, "The Collection: People: Arthur Welsh"; see also "Arthur Welsh, 1881–1912," available at http://www.earlyaviators.com/ewelsh. The website cites Laura Apelbaum and the Jewish Historical Society, plus "Jewish Aviator and Pilot to be Honored," *Chronicle* 66, 5 (December 2003) for the information.

206 "Begin Work at Camp," *Montgomery Advertiser,* April 18, 1910, p. 6. The *Montgomery Advertiser* incorrectly identified Arthur L. Welsh as "L. N. Welch." For more on Welsh's background, see Crouch, p. 427.

207 "Wright Again Mounts Aloft," *Montgomery Advertiser,* April 22, 1910, p. 10.

208 "With Ease He Navigates Air," *Montgomery Advertiser,* April 23, 1910, p. 7.

209 Ibid.

210 Ibid.

211 Flynt, p. 73.

212 "Urges Visits to See Wright," *Montgomery Advertiser,* April 24, 1910, p. 27. The bracketed material "[of seeing]" replaces an archaic, garbled phrase in the original. Cassels clearly meant he was watching the flight.

213 "Urges Visits to See Wright," *Montgomery Advertiser,* April 24, 1910, p. 27.

214 Ibid.

215 "Cold Wave Carries Ruin Before it Through South," *Montgomery Advertiser*, April 26, 1910, p. 1.

216 Ibid.

217 "Aviators Forsake Training to Secure Views in Snow Storm," *Montgomery Advertiser*, April 26, 1910, p. 2.

218 Ibid.

219 "Wright Makes Local Record," *Montgomery Advertiser*, April 27, 1910, p. 9.

220 Associated Press, "Paulhan Wins $50,000 Prize," *Montgomery Advertiser*, April 28, 1910, p. 1.

221 "Wright Meets with Accident," *Montgomery Advertiser*, April 28, 1910, p. 10.

222 Associated Press, "Accident in San Antonio," *Montgomery Advertiser*, April 28, 1910, p. 10.

223 Wayne Greenhaw, *Montgomery: The Biography of a City* (Montgomery, Ala.: The Advertiser Company, 1993), p. 75.

224 "Wright Meets with Accident," *Montgomery Advertiser*, April 28, 1910, p. 10.

225 "Wright Mounts High Into Air," *Montgomery Advertiser*, April 29, 1910, p. 5. The crowd total is given in "Wilbur and Orville Wright: A Chronology, 1910, Montgomery, Ala.," available at http://www.centennialofflight.gov/chrono/log/1910MontgomeryAla.htm.

226 "Wright Makes Fine Flight in Machine," *Birmingham Age-Herald*, April 29, 1910, p. 3.

227 Ennels and Newton, p. 17. Their estimate was a rough one in general, not for any particular day.

228 "Great Crowds Watch Wright," *Montgomery Advertiser*, May 1, 1910, p. 27.

229 Associated Press, "Flies Over War Ships," *Montgomery Advertiser*, May 1, 1910, p. 27.

230 "[Torn] Wright and his Quintet of Pupils As They Appear at Work at Training Camp," *Montgomery Advertiser*, May 2, 1910, p. 2.

231 "Wright Takes Kohn With Him," *Montgomery Advertiser*, May 4, 1910, p. 8.

232 Ibid.

233 Owen, III, p. 84.

234 "Wright Takes Kohn With Him," *Montgomery Advertiser*, May 4, 1910, p. 8.

235 Ibid.

236 Ibid.

237 Ibid.

238 Quoted in Ennels and Newton, p. 17.

239 Ball, in U.S. Army, *Maxwell Field: Army Air Corps*, pp. 11–12. In his narrative, Ball does not mention making up the missed flight opportunity.

240 "Wright Takes Kohn With Him," *Montgomery Advertiser*, May 4, 1910, p. 8.

## Chapter 5—The Students and the Student Teacher

241 "Wright Not to Abandon Camp," *Montgomery Advertiser*, May 5, 1910, p. 7.

242 "Wright Not to Abandon Camp," *Montgomery Advertiser*, May 5, 1910, p. 7.

243 Ennels and Newton, p. 17.

244 "Crowds of Montgomerians See Orville Wright as He Pilots Aeroplane Into Skies," *Montgomery Advertiser*, May 6, 1910, p. 7.

245 Ibid.

246 Ibid.

247 Ibid.

248 Ibid.

249 "Wright Smiles and Goes Away," *Montgomery Advertiser*, May 8, 1910, p. 16.

250 Ibid.

251 "Bi-Plane in Accident," *Montgomery Advertiser*, May 10, 1910, p. 7; also "Aeroplane Repaired; Flights Again Thursday," *Montgomery Advertiser*, May 11, 1910, p. 5.

252 Associated Press, "Unconscious Aeronauts," *Montgomery Advertiser*, May 11, 1910, p. 11.

253 Associated Press, "Gas Envelope Was Torn Open," *Montgomery Advertiser*, May 12, 1910, p. 1.

254 "Right Plane is Broken," *Montgomery Advertiser*, May 14, 1910, p. 9.

255 Ibid.

256 "Will Abandon Aviation Camp," *Montgomery Advertiser*, May 22, 1910, p. 24.

257 Ibid.

258 Ibid.

259 Associated Press, "Highest Up In The Air," *Montgomery Advertiser*, May 13, 1910, p. 8.

260 Associated Press, "Took Children Up," *Montgomery Advertiser*, May 20, 1910, p. 10.

261 "Boys Fly for Record," *Montgomery Advertiser*, May 24, 1910, p. 5.

262 See, for example, "Great Crowds Watch Wright," *Montgomery Advertiser*, May 1, 1910, p. 27.

263 "Boys Fly for Record," *Montgomery Advertiser*, May 24, 1910, p. 5.

264 "Aviator Flies All Round Montgomery by Moonlight," *Birmingham Age-Herald*, May 26, 1910, p. 1.

265 "Boys Fly for Record," *Montgomery Advertiser*, May 24, 1910, p. 5.

266 "Aeroplane Driven In Midnight Sky," *Montgomery Advertiser*, May 26, 1910, p. 3. Although these flights were acclaimed in the *Montgomery Advertiser* as the first true night flights, Wilbur flew into a moonlit dusk shortly before, according to Harris, p. 116. Harris acknowledges that Wilbur's flight did not prove that an airplane could land in darkness—something Brookins and Hoxsey did prove in Montgomery. And, as the *Montgomery Advertiser* noted, the Montgomery night flights marked the first time (at least, the first time in America) that pilots had deliberately chosen the night hours for flight, as opposed to simply completing a day flight after dusk. See "Aviation Camp was a Success," *Montgomery Advertiser*, May 30, 1910, p. 8. For years, Hoxsey and Brookins were credited with the first true night flights in the world. Various Internet sources now claim that French pilot Emil Aubrun made the first night flight in Villalaguno, near Buenos Aires, Argentina, on March 10, 1910. Aubrun's name appears in several lists of important dates regarding aviation in 1910, but with no elaboration whatsoever on the flight. If the lists are accurate, then Hoxsey and Brookins made the first American night flights, not the first such flights in the world. In any case, any such flight by Aubrun was unknown in America in May 1910 when Brookins and Hoxsey took to the night sky in Montgomery. For the scant information available on Aubrun, see "The Beginnings of Flight, 1903–1910," available at http://cnparm.home.texas.net/Subj/Flight/Flight01.htm. See also "1910 in Aviation," http://www.answers.com/topic/1910-in-aviation, plus "Wright Brothers Aeroplane Company: The Pioneers," available at http://www.wright-brothers.org/History/History%20of%20Airplane/the_pioneers.htm.

267 "Aeroplane Driven In Midnight Sky," *Montgomery Advertiser*, May 26, 1910, p. 3.

268 Ibid.

269 Ibid.

270 "Will Abandon Aviation Camp," *Montgomery Advertiser*, May 22, 1910, p. 24.

271 "Aviation Camp is Abandoned," *Montgomery Advertiser*, May 28, 1910, p. 5. Howard, p. 360, says the exhibition team debuted in the Indianapolis meet.

272 "Aviation Camp is Abandoned," *Montgomery Advertiser*, May 28, 1910, p. 5.

273 Ibid.

274 "Big Aeroplane Shipped North," *Montgomery Advertiser*, May 29, 1910, p. 7.

275 "Aviation Camp was a Success," *Montgomery Advertiser*, May 30, 1910, p. 8.

276 Ibid. For one indication of popular thought that associated aviation with sports, see Associated Press, "Burgess Thinks He Has Conquered The Air," *Montgomery Advertiser's* sports page, May 13, 1910, p. 11.

277 "Aviation Camp was a Success," *Montgomery Advertiser*, May 30, 1910, p. 8.

278 Ibid.

279 Ibid.

280 Ibid. The article mistakenly said "universally low temperatures," but it was clear from the rest of the paragraph, discussing cold and wind in other sections of the United States, that the reporter meant "warm" temperatures.

281 "Aviation Camp was a Success," *Montgomery Advertiser*, May 30, 1910, p. 8.

282 Ibid.

283 Untitled, unsigned lead editorial, *Montgomery Advertiser*, May 31, 1910, p. 4. Paulhan's plans were detailed in "Paulhan Plans London-Paris Aerial Flight," *Montgomery Advertiser*, May 11, 1910, p. 12.

284 See, for example, Associated Press, "Makes High Flight Mark," *Montgomery Advertiser*, June 14, 1910, p. 1.

285 Associated Press, "Man-Bird Curtiss High Over Hudson Glides to Gotham," *Montgomery Advertiser*, May 30, 1910, p. 1.

286 Associated Press, "Over Channel and Back Again," *Montgomery Advertiser*, June 3, 1910, p. 1; see also Harris, p. 140 on the Rolls-Royce connection.

287 Untitled, unsigned lead editorial, *Montgomery Advertiser*, June 4, 1910, p. 4.

288 Associated Press, "Wrights Will Enter," *Montgomery Advertiser*, June 3, 1910, p. 1.

289 Associated Press, "Over Channel and Back Again," *Montgomery Advertiser*, June 3, 1910, p. 1.

290 Associated Press, "All Ready for Aviation Meet," *Montgomery Advertiser*, June 13, 1910, p. 1.

291 Associated Press, "Makes High Flight Mark," *Montgomery Advertiser*, June 14, 1910, p. 1.

292 Associated Press, "Hamilton Makes City-To-City Flight," *Montgomery Advertiser*, June 14, 1910, p. 1.

293 Associated Press, "Hamilton Will Enter Chicago-New York Race," *Montgomery Advertiser*, June 17, 1910, p. 1.

294 Associated Press, "New York to St. Louis," *Montgomery Advertiser*, June 1, 1910, p. 1.

295 Associated Press, "Aeroplane Makes Big Drop; Driver Not Hurt," *Montgomery Advertiser*, June 17, 1910, p. 1.

296 Walter R. Brookins, quoted in Harris, p. 122. Unfortunately, in regards to Brookins's description of the climbing rate of a "good ship today," the interview with Brookins was undated.

297 Associated Press, "Aeroplane Makes Big Drop; Driver Not Hurt," *Montgomery Advertiser*, June 17, 1910, p. 1.

## Chapter 6—Whatever Happened to the Class of 1910?

298 Associated Press, "Curtiss Breaks Record," *Montgomery Advertiser*, June 19, 1910, p. 1.

299 Gilbert Edge, "Howdy!" (cartoon), *Montgomery Advertiser*, May 11, 1910, p. 4.

300 Associated Press, "Paulhan Plans London-Paris Aerial Flight," *Montgomery Advertiser*, May 11, 1910, p. 12.

301 Associated Press, "Forty Minutes Across the Channel," *Montgomery Advertiser*, May 22, 1910, p. 1.

302 Untitled, unsigned editorial, *Montgomery Advertiser*, May 23, 1910, p. 4.

303 Untitled, unsigned editorial, *Montgomery Advertiser*, May 26, 1910, p. 4.

304 Associated Press, "Young French Aviator Killed in a Race," *Montgomery Advertiser*, May 14, 1910, p. 1.

305 Associated Press, "Aeroplane Causes Panic," *Montgomery Advertiser*, May 29, 1910, p. 12.

306 Associated Press, "Ten-Year-Old Boy Carried Into Clouds," *Montgomery Advertiser*, June 16, 1910, p. 1.

307 Unsigned editorial, "Dirigible Gown Now," *Montgomery Advertiser*, May 25, 1910, p. 4.

308 For example, see the picture of Katharine Wright in an airplane, skirts tied, number 52, p. 62, in Orville Wright, *How We Invented The Airplane.*

309 "What the Airship Will Be In The Next Five Years," *Montgomery Advertiser*, May 12, 1910, p. 4; reprinted from "Over Sea by Airship," *Century*, May 1910.

310 Associated Press, "English Army Airship Makes Midnight Trip," *Montgomery Advertiser*, June 5, 1910, p. 1.

311 Unsigned editorial, "Registering Airships," *Montgomery Advertiser*, June 6, 1910, p. 4.

312 Associated Press, "Strange Airship Seen In The Ohio Skies," *Montgomery Advertiser*, March 23, 1910, p. 6.

313 Associated Press, "Burgess Thinks He Has Conquered The Air," *Montgomery Advertiser*, May 13, 1910, p. 11.

314 Associated Press, "War Kites That Carry Men Are Giving Good Results," *Montgomery Advertiser*, May 22, 1910, p. 10.

315 This will be detailed shortly. See Ennels and Newton, pp. 17–19.

316 Associated Press, "Man-Bird Curtiss High Over Hudson Glides to Gotham," *Montgomery Advertiser*, May 30, 1910, p. 1.

317 Associated Press, "The Victorious Man-Bird Curtiss as He Landed Big Prize," *Montgomery Advertiser*, June 1, 1910, p. 16.

318 Associated Press, "College Men as Aeronauts," *Montgomery Advertiser*, May 23, 1910, p. 1.

319 Ibid.

320 "Holtzclaw Medal Prize," *Montgomery Advertiser*, June 5, 1910, p. 29.

321 "Victory Over Air is Now Achieved," *Birmingham Age-Herald*, May 29, 1910, p. 1.

322 Ibid.

323 OhioLINK Digital Media Center, Historic and Archival Collections, photo of Hoxsey's crash into the grandstands, available at http://dmc.ohiolink.edu, Wright Brothers Collection, keyword "Hoxsey." See also Stanley W. Kandebo, "The Wright Brothers and the Birth of an Industry," *Aviation Week & Space Technology,* December 30, 2002, originally accessed at *Aviation Week's The Next Century of Flight,* http://www.aviationw. com/content/ncof. That site is no longer active, but the article is available from The U.S. Department of Transportation, TRIS Online at http://ntlsearch.bts.gov/tris/record/

tris/00947213.html.

324 United Press, "TR's flight was risky, flyer says," reprinted from *Cleveland Press* (Ohio), October 12, 1910, available at http://100years.upi.com/sta_1910-10-12.html. An amazing newsreel of the flight, which featured frighteningly steep dives near the ground, is available at http://www.wrightexperience.com/edu/film/html/5525015LgMv.htm. The story of the flight, as follows in the next several paragraphs, comes from the *Cleveland Press* news account and the newsreel.

325 Howard, p. 356, and Crouch, p. 431.

326 Wilbur Wright to Arch Hoxsey, September 19, 1910, quoted in Howard, p. 353.

327 *New York American,* January 1, 1911, reprinted in Scott, p. 181. Other details supplied by Harris, p. 160.

328 Howard, p. 360.

329 See a Mecca Cigarettes trading card of Hoxsey at "Archibald 'Arch' Hoxsey, 1884–1910," at http://www.earlyaviators.com/ehoxsey.htm.

330 Howard, p. 360.

331 Howard, pp. 353, 360.

332 Frank Coffyn Collection, "The Collection: People: Arthur Welsh," and "Arthur Welsh, 1881–1912," noted in "Jewish Aviator and Pilot to be Honored," *Chronicle.*

333 Howard, p. 361. Also see Stimson, "Wright Model C: End of the Line," site archives in subsection "Wright Activities after 1903"; also see "Arthur Welsh, 1881–1912" at http://www.earlyaviators.com/ewelsh.htm. The website quotes "Two Airmen Are Killed; Lieut. L. W. Hazelhurst and A. L. Welch [*sic*] the Victims," *Chattanooga Daily Times* (Tennessee), June 12, 1912.

334 Harris, pp. 117–118, 159. See also Howard, p. 360.

335 Walter R. Brookins, undated, quoted in Harris, pp. 151–152.

336 Walter R. Brookins, undated, quoted in Harris, pp. 137–138.

337 Roger E. Bilstein, "The Airplane, The Wrights, and The American Public," pp. 39–51 in Hallion, pp. 45–46. According to Bilstein, the clip is in the Library of Congress.

338 Milton Wright, diary entry, May 30, 1912. Bishop Wright's many diary entries about Wilbur's final illness are quoted in Kirk, pp. 257–258. The quoted material is on p. 258.

339 Brochure reprinted in Stimson, "Wright Company Flying School." Stimson did not give the formal title of the brochure.

340 Ibid.

341 See, for example, Associated Press, "For Aeroplane Factory Here, *"Montgomery Advertiser,* February 20, 1910, p. 28. See also "The Wright Aeroplane Test in North Carolina," *Scientific American* XCVIII (May 30, 1908): 393.

342 For example, "First Flights of the Aerial Experiment Association's Second Aeroplane," *Scientific American* XCVIII (May 30, 1908): 392, juxtaposed with "The Wright Aeroplane Test in North Carolina," on p. 393 of the same issue.

343 Washington, D.C., *Evening Star*, quoted in Harris, p. 100.

344 The further history of the Wrights' flying field is derived from Ennels and Newton, pp. 17–19.

345 Ennels and Newton, pp. 21–27.

346 Ennels and Newton, pp. 21–27; plus references to the Air University throughout chapters 5, 6, and 7, particularly pp. 117–119 and 177. The reference to Orville's visit is on p. 195, note 2. Ennels and Newton describe the training facility Orville visited in World War II as "the aerodrome for heavy and very heavy bomber transitional training."

347 Major W. R. Weaver, "Foreword," to U.S. Army, *Maxwell Field: Army Air Corps*, p. 5.

## Photograph and Illustration Sources

Cover images (except trolleys) and all images not mentioned below are from the hold-
ings of Maxwell Air Force Base's Air Force Historical Research Agency, Montgomery,
Alabama.

Cover (Trolleys): Alabama Power Co., Birmingham, Alabama (APC).

Chapter 1: Page 22, APC. Page 23, APC. Page 28, Gilbert Edge, *Montgomery Advertiser*,
Montgomery, Alabama (MA), February 2, 1910, p. 4. Page 34, Edge, MA, January 30,
1910, p. 4. Page 36, Edge, MA, January 14, 1910, p. 4.

Chapter 2: Page 49, Edge, MA, February 24, 1910, p. 4. Page 57, Montgomery Fair, MA,
March 20, 1910, p. 28, and March 25, 1910, p. 9.

Chapter 6: Page 118, Edge, MA, May 11, 1910, p. 4. Page 123, MA, May 13, 1910, p. 11.
Page 127, Historic Print & Map Co., St. Augustine, Florida.

# INDEX

only student devoted entirely to pilot
instruction, 130
trained Hap Arnold, who ran air op-
erations in World War II, 130
"Whirlwinds," 79–80, 85–86
"White Wing" (airplane), 31
Wilbur. *See* Wright, Wilbur
William, Duke of Normandy, 120
Winds, 32, 39, 44, 72, 78–79, 86, 91,
105–106, 109–110, 112, 129, 134.
*See also* "Whirlwinds"
Wing-warping, 18, 29–30, 125
"With Wright" (cartoon of "Miss Montgomery"), 48–49
Women and flying, 83–84, 121
Woodlawn (Birmingham suburb), 34,
119
World War I, 126, 137–139
World War II, 139
Wright bicycle shop, 66
Wright brothers, 63, 86, 107–108, 123,
130, 133, 137, 139–140. *See also*
Wright, Wilbur; Wright, Orville
announce they'll leave Montgomery,
93
arrival in Montgomery, 15
as inventors of airplane, 52, 107, 113
as newspapermen, 18
claim of flight widely doubted at first,
30
expect others to carry on after them,
14, 100, 109, 111, 133–134
license other airplanes, 31–32, 75–76,
85
magicians in public relations, 135–137
patents, 14, 29–31
relationship to Montgomery, 111–112
say they no longer fly for money, 62,
64
secrecy, 30, 32, 135
teaching military officers to fly, 14, 52
wooed by Commercial Club, 43
Wright Company, 38, 41, 53, 58, 60,
67, 80, 84, 95, 130, 132

Wright Company School of Aviation
(Dayton), 134
Wright Exhibition Company/exhibition
team, 14, 108, 129
"Wright Flyer" (airplane). *See* "Flyer"
Wright, Katharine, 66
Wright, Orville, 31, 68–69, 71, 73–74,
86, 89, 91, 110–111, 114, 116–117,
123–124, 133, 137
arrives in Montgomery, 64
attempts to improve public relations,
67
attends Indianapolis meet, 114
bachelor Orville with flirtatious girl,
99–100
dapper dresser, 64–65
described as uncooperative, 47
eventually cooperates with city desire
for publicity, 134
fancy flying repertoire, 87–90, 93, 99
fatal crash (talks about), 70, 75
first pilot, 13, 17
glides safely to ground in mishap, 92
horrified about "Model C," 130
imminent departure, 97–98
leaves Montgomery, 100
likes Montgomery, 83, 100–101
locates and identifies Venus, 82
orders students to Dayton, 108
patent issues, 31
plans to teach pilots, 42
praised as a pilot by Frank Kohn, 96
praised by *Age-Herald*, 68–69
praised for skill, 79, 86
praises citizens of Montgomery for
their energy, 83
praises Montgomery as picturesque,
83
"Professor of Flying," 13, 84, 86
returns from Ohio trip, ready to repair
airplane, 86
sets up school, 15
spectators prefer him to Brookins,
98–99